CONTACT GRILL

Bridget Jones

CONTACT GRILL

HAMLYN

London · New York · Sydney · Toronto

DEDICATION

To Neill – who enjoys a good grilling!

The author and publisher would
like to thank the following for their
help with this book:
Electricity Council
Moulinex Limited
Pifco
Rima Electric Limited
Sunbeam Electric Limited
Sutherlands Spreads, Quaker Oats Limited
Tefal UK Limited

Photography by Paul Kemp
Line illustrations by Ian Beck and Ron Hayward

Published by
The Hamlyn Publishing Group Limited
London · New York · Sydney · Toronto
Astronaut House, Feltham, Middlesex, England
© Copyright The Hamlyn Publishing Group Limited 1982

ISBN 0 600 32275 0

Set in 10 on 12pt Monophoto Rockwell Light
by Photocomp Limited, Birmingham, England

Printed in Italy

Contents

Useful facts and figures

Notes on metrication

In this book quantities are given in metric and Imperial measures. Exact conversion from Imperial to metric measures does not usually give very convenient working quantities and so the metric measures have been rounded off into units of 25 grams. The table below shows the recommended equivalents.

Ounces	Approx g to nearest whole figure	Recommended conversion to nearest unit of 25	Ounces	Approx g to nearest whole figure	Recommended conversion to nearest unit of 25
1	28	25	11	312	300
2	57	50	12	340	350
3	85	75	13	368	375
4	113	100	14	396	400
5	142	150	15	425	425
6	170	175	16 (1 lb)	454	450
7	198	200	17	482	475
8	227	225	18	510	500
9	255	250	19	539	550
10	283	275	20 (1¼ lb)	567	575

Note: When converting quantities over 20 oz first add the appropriate figures in the centre column, then adjust to the nearest unit of 25. As a general guide, 1 kg (1000 g) equals 2.2 lb or about 2 lb 3 oz. This method of conversion gives good results in nearly all cases, although in certain pastry and cake recipes a more accurate conversion is necessary to produce a balanced recipe.

Liquid measures The millilitre has been used in this book and the following table gives a few examples.

Imperial	Approx ml to nearest whole figure	Recommended ml	Imperial	Approx ml to nearest whole figure	Recommended ml
¼ pint	142	150 ml	1 pint	567	600 ml
½ pint	283	300 ml	1½ pints	851	900 ml
¾ pint	425	450 ml	1¾ pints	992	1000 ml (1 litre)

Spoon measures All spoon measures given in this book are level unless otherwise stated.

Can sizes At present, cans are marked with the exact (usually to the nearest whole number) metric equivalent of the Imperial weight of the contents, so we have followed this practice when giving can sizes.

Notes for American and Australian users

In America the 8-oz measuring cup is used. In Australia metric measures are now used in conjunction with the standard 250-ml measuring cup. The Imperial pint, used in Britain and Australia, is 20 fl oz, while the American pint is 16 fl oz. It is important to remember that the Australian tablespoon differs from both the British and American tablespoons; the table below gives a comparison. The British standard tablespoon, which has been used throughout this book, holds 17.7 ml, the American 14.2 ml, and the Australian 20 ml. A teaspoon holds approximately 5 ml in all three countries.

British	American	Australian
1 teaspoon	1 teaspoon	1 teaspoon
1 tablespoon	1 tablespoon	1 tablespoon
2 tablespoons	3 tablespoons	2 tablespoons
3½ tablespoons	4 tablespoons	3 tablespoons
4 tablespoons	5 tablespoons	3½ tablespoons

An Imperial/American guide to solid and liquid measures

Imperial	American	Imperial	American
Solid measures		**Liquid measures**	
1 lb butter or		¼ pint liquid	⅝ cup liquid
margarine	2 cups	½ pint	1¼ cups
1 lb flour	4 cups	¾ pint	2 cups
1 lb granulated		1 pint	2½ cups
or castor sugar	2 cups	1½ pints	3¾ cups
1 lb icing sugar	3 cups	2 pints	5 cups (2½
8 oz rice	1 cup		pints)

Note: When making any of the recipes in this book, only follow one set of measures as they are not interchangeable.

American terms

The list below gives some American equivalents or substitutes for terms and ingredients used in this book.

British/American	British/American
cling film/Saran wrap	black olives/ripe olives
cocktail stick/toothpick	courgettes/zucchini
cooking foil/aluminium foil	spring onion/scallion
greaseproof paper/waxed paper	sugar, icing/confectioner's sugar
top and tail/stem and head	yogurt, natural/yogurt, plain

Introduction

I first bought a contact grill for cooking quick suppers when I arrived home late from work and for making toasted sandwiches when friends called unexpectedly. But it was when I moved house and found myself with spartan kitchen facilities that my contact grill really came into its own.

For six months I cooked all our meals, gave small dinner parties for friends and entertained my parents-in-law with the sole aid of my faithful contact grill and a tiny camping stove. During this time I developed many of the recipe ideas that are included in this book and these have all been thoroughly tested since in other contact grills of various kinds.

Even though I now have a well-equipped kitchen I still find that my contact grill is the quickest and most economical way of cooking dinner for two. Whether you live in a small bedsit or enjoy the facilities of a large family kitchen I'm sure that you, too, will find it an indispensable piece of equipment and that you'll soon come to wonder how you ever managed without one!

Bridget L. Jones

About your grill

Grilling is a quick, efficient method of cooking which needs no additional fat. The food retains its full nutritional value and loses none of its flavour. It is also very economical, as cooking times are comparatively short.

With the increase of home entertaining and the growing interest in quick, casual meals, portable cooking appliances have become especially popular and the most versatile of these is the contact grill. Originally known as infra-red grills, they were first introduced in catering establishments, but smaller versions for domestic use are now widely available and there is an attractive range to choose from. They are finished in bright enamel or polished chrome and stand firmly on insulated feet so that they can be safely used on most surfaces.

How it works

The contact grill consists of two heavy aluminium heating plates generating infra-red heat which come in direct contact with the food, cooking it rapidly on both sides by direct conduction. These plates vary in size according to the make, ranging from about 18 × 20 cm to 30 × 30 cm. Both plates have ribbed surfaces which assist the radiation of the infra-red heat and help to seal the food quickly, ensuring that it is thoroughly cooked. The plates are usually coated with a non-stick substance such as Teflon for easy cleaning, and in some models they can be removed and washed or exchanged for alternative sets.

The top plate has an open hinge which is adjustable to allow for foods of varying thickness, and some models are supplied with a shallow baking tray with a lever to hold it in position. Some models have a 'lift and lock' height adjustment. If your contact grill does not include a baking tray, a square baking tin about 3·5 / 1½ inches deep would be a suitable alternative for cooking soft foods. In

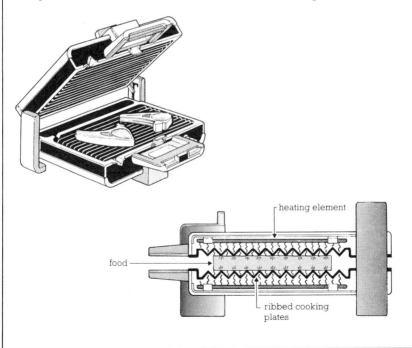

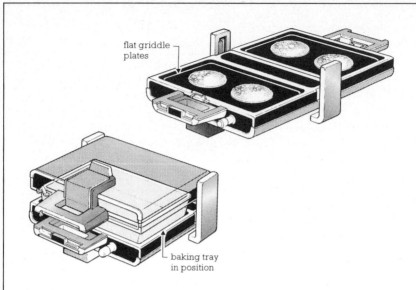

flat griddle plates

baking tray in position

some models it is possible to open the lid out flat to double the heating area and form a griddle with the ribbed plates reversed to give a flat surface.

Controls

Depending on the size of your contact grill, the total loading of both plates varies between 1 kw and 2 kw and the apparatus can be connected to any earthed 13-amp socket outlet. Sandwich and waffle makers do not have variable heat settings: there is just a thermostat to ensure that the appliance does not overheat. Most contact grills, however, have three to five preset thermostat positions ranging in temperature from 100 to 300 c (212 to 572 f), depending on the model, and in this book the recipes refer either to the lowest, medium or hottest settings. For an appliance with five settings these would correspond to 1 for the lowest setting, 3 for the middle, and 5 would be the hottest setting in the temperature range. Most recipes require the hottest setting, though a few call for the medium, and the lowest temperature is generally suitable for keeping food hot for a short time or for reheating food slowly from a cold or frozen condition. For a breakdown of the setting temperatures and timing requirements of individual foods, see the cooking chart on page 14.

How to use it

The cooking times given for the different recipes in this book refer to the time taken to cook the dish once the grill has reached the temperature recommended by the manufacturer. Most models have a light which glows as soon as the main switch is turned on and goes out when the correct cooking temperature has been reached. This preheating time can vary from 3 to 12 minutes, depending on the size or age of your appliance, but if the food is not quite prepared by the time your contact grill is ready to cook it, don't worry – the thermostat control will prevent the grill from overheating.

Once the correct temperature has been reached, the actual cooking time is very short indeed. For some recipes it is so brief that it needs to be very precise, and it is advisable to use a timer or to keep a close eye on the clock while cooking. It is important to follow strictly the manufacturer's instructions for each particular model, especially with regard to the preheating times. A general guide to timing for a range of foods will be found in our cooking chart on page 14.

Before you use your contact grill for the first time brush the cooking plates lightly with oil. When the grill has been preheated and the correct temperature reached, place the prepared food on the bottom plate and lower the top so that both plates are in direct contact with the food. To achieve this, the pieces of food must be of uniform thickness, and it may be necessary to remove protruding bones from chops and cutlets. Once the grill is hot, different items can be cooked in succession and, if necessary, turned over halfway through the cooking time. A channel running round the edge of the cooking plates with a lip on one side collects melted fat, and if you are cooking food with a high fat content, such as pork chops, it's a good idea to place a small container under the lip to catch any drips.

Not only chops can be grilled successfully. Toasted sandwiches with various fillings can be quickly made, or ready-prepared frozen sandwiches may be taken straight from the freezer and grilled to give you a quick snack. For this purpose a cheese filling is ideal. Other fillings containing meat can also be used, but they may need a longer cooking time at a slower setting to ensure that the filling has reached a sufficiently high temperature to be thoroughly heated through. Chops and steaks may be cooked from the frozen state and some individual frozen meals in shallow aluminium trays may be quickly thawed and reheated on your contact grill. Using the special tray, you can also bake scones, biscuits and small pastry items or reheat ready-cooked and frozen baked foods.

Caring for it

Switch off after cooking, unplug the grill and with the lid raised, leave it to cool. Before it is quite cold, wipe the plates with absorbent kitchen paper to remove excess fat before it congeals, picking off any food particles. If you don't do this, next time you switch on the grill it will smoke unpleasantly as the fat heats up and burns off. Some grills are supplied with a wooden scraper, or you can use a wooden or nylon spatula to clean the plates. Metal utensils should never be used, or you may damage the non-stick coating. Detachable plates can be soaked in hot, soapy water, or a nylon brush dipped in a hot detergent solution will remove burnt-on scraps of food. The grill itself, of course, should never be immersed in water. You can, if you like, line the heating plates with cooking foil to protect them from spattering fat – the heat efficiency will not be affected.

A quick wipe with absorbent kitchen paper or a clean cloth is all that is needed to clean the outside.

Play safe

★ Always follow the manufacturer's instructions when using your appliance.

★ Make sure your contact grill is standing on a firm, heat-resistant surface near a power point, and that there is plenty of room beside it on which to dish up the hot food.

★ When the cooking time is up, open your grill with care. It will be very hot and the food will be steaming – oven gloves are a useful protection.

★ Be sure to switch off and unplug your contact grill after use. Don't attempt to remove the plates for cleaning until they are cool enough to handle.

(Based on information supplied by the Electricity Council)

GRILLS

Mention a contact grill and the first image that springs to mind is a succulent juicy chop, hamburger or chicken piece. These foods are particularly suitable for grilling. Even when frozen they can be cooked in a fraction of the usual time and, thanks to the high degree of heat generated and rapidity of the cooking, all the rich juices will be sealed in to retain the full flavour of the meat. And the time doesn't vary, however much you cook at once – six sausages take no longer than one.

For some of the most popular foods, check our chart on the following pages to find the right balance of time and temperature settings.

Cooking chart

Food	Preparation	Grilling plate/ cooking tray	Cooking time in minutes	Cooking time from frozen
Chicken drumsticks or small, evenly shaped joints – 75-100 g/3-4 oz each	Season lightly and wrap in cooking foil	grilling plates	20	frozen chicken not recommended
Chops: lamb – 100 g/4 oz each	brush with oil and season lightly	grilling plates	10	add 15 minutes
pork – 175 g/6 oz each	choose chops with small bones	grilling plates	8	add 1-2 minutes
Fish: cakes (frozen)	—	cooking tray	—	10 minutes
fillets – 175 g/ 6 oz	season lightly and dot with butter	cooking tray	10–12	add 5–8 minutes
fingers – (frozen)	—	cooking tray	—	10 minutes
whole, medium-sized fish such as trout, mackerel or herring	gut, season and dot with butter	cooking tray	15	add 10–15 minutes
Gammon steaks 225 g/8 oz	—	grilling plates	4–5	add 6–10 minutes
Hamburgers: 225 g/8 oz	brush with a little oil	grilling plates	5–10	add 2–5 minutes
100 g/4 oz	brush with a little oil	grilling plates	4–8	add 1–3 minutes
Lamb, boned breast	trim excess fat, season well and place flat in tray	cooking tray	30–40	frozen lamb not recommended
Oven chips (frozen, part cooked) – 225 g/ 8 oz	—	cooking tray	—	15 minutes

Food	Preparation	Grilling plate/ cooking tray	Cooking time in minutes	Cooking time from frozen
Pies, individual – chicken/steak and kidney (frozen uncooked)	—	cooking tray	—	35 minutes
Pizza, individual (frozen uncooked)	—	cooking tray	—	10 minutes
Sausages: chipolata	—	cooking tray	8	add 5–7 minutes
thick	—	cooking tray	15	add 5 minutes
Sausage rolls, large (frozen uncooked)	—	cooking tray	—	25–30 minutes
Steak: fillet – 175 g/6 oz	brush with a little oil, season lightly	grilling plates	3–8	add 5–7 minutes
rump – 225 g/ 8 oz	brush with a little oil, season lightly	grilling plates	4–10	add 3–5 minutes
Toasted sandwiches	see pages 112-6	grilling or sandwich plates	3	add 2–4 minutes
Veal escalope 175 g/6 oz	brush with a little oil, season lightly	grilling plates	2–3	add 1–2 minutes

Individual mixed grill

(Illustrated on page 33)
Temperature: hottest setting · Serves: 1

2 lean bacon rashers, rind removed
75 g/3 oz lamb's liver, sliced
1 lamb chop
1 thick pork sausage
salt and freshly ground black pepper
25 g/1 oz butter
1 tomato, halved
4-6 mushrooms

Roll the bacon rashers and secure with wooden cocktail sticks. Place in the cooking tray with the liver, lamb chop and sausage. Season to taste and dot with the butter. Cook on the hottest setting for 15 minutes. Add the halved tomato and mushrooms for the last 2 minutes of the cooking time.

Shepherd's grill

Temperature: hottest setting · Serves: 2

2 lamb cutlets
50 g/2 oz button mushrooms
4 lamb's kidneys, halved and cored
50 g/2 oz butter
salt and freshly ground black pepper
2 tomatoes, halved
2 tablespoons chopped parsley

Wipe the cutlets and mushrooms and arrange in the cooking tray with the kidneys. Dot with the butter and season generously. Cook on the hottest setting for 15 minutes, adding the tomatoes for the last 2 minutes of the cooking time. Sprinkle with chopped parsley and serve immediately.

Kidney and bacon grill

(Illustrated on page 33)
Temperature: hottest setting · Serves: 2

4 lamb's kidneys, cored
4 lean bacon rashers, rind removed
50 g/2 oz butter
1 teaspoon French mustard
2 medium-thick slices bread
2 small tomatoes

Wrap each kidney in a bacon rasher and place in the cooking tray. Cream the butter with the mustard and spread on both sides of the bread. Arrange the bread in the cooking tray with the kidneys and cook on the hottest setting for 10-12 minutes, turning the bread once during cooking. Cut a small cross with a sharp knife in the top of each tomato and place in the cooking tray for the last 2 minutes of the cooking time.

Pork and apple grill

Temperature: hottest setting · Serves: 2

2 pork chops
1 eating apple, cored and sliced
1 onion, sliced
2 sprigs fresh sage
2 chipolata sausages
50 g/2 oz butter
salt and freshly ground black pepper

Place the chops in the cooking tray with the sliced apple and onion. Top with the sage and add the sausages. Dot with the butter and season generously. Cook on the hottest setting for 25 minutes. Serve with creamed or new potatoes.

Steak and onion grill

Temperature: hottest setting · Serves: 2

The cooking time in this recipe gives a medium to well-done steak and allows enough time for the potatoes to cook. If rare steak is required, the potatoes should be cooked for 10 minutes before the steak is added.

1 (350-g/12-oz) piece rump steak
1 onion, sliced
2 bay leaves
50 g/2 oz button mushrooms
1 large potato, peeled and thinly sliced
50 g/2 oz butter
salt and freshly ground black pepper

Trim the steak and place in the cooking tray. Top with the onion slices and bay leaves. Arrange the mushrooms and potato in the tray and dot with the butter. Season and cook on the hottest setting for 25 minutes. Serve the steak, halved, with a crisp green salad.

Finnan haddie and egg grill

Temperature: hottest setting · Serves: 2

2 (175-g/6-oz) smoked haddock fillets
50 g/2 oz butter
2 eggs
salt and freshly ground black pepper

Wipe the haddock fillets and place in the cooking tray. Dot with the butter. Cook on the hottest setting for 5 minutes. Break the eggs carefully into the tray with the haddock, season lightly and cook for a further 2 minutes. Remove to heated plates and serve immediately with thin slices of brown bread and butter.

FISH &
SEAFOOD

The speed with which fish cooks in a contact grill ensures that neither flavour nor moisture is lost. Crisp coatings stay crunchy, fresh fish remains firm, and with an imaginative recipe even the blandest fish can be transformed into a gourmet dish.

Whether you are using whole fish or fillets, fresh or frozen, the delicious recipes that follow for various kinds of seafood reflect the wide range of possibilities your contact grill can tackle.

White fish and bacon grill

Temperature: hottest setting · Serves: 2

Fish steaks as well as fillets may be used in this dish.

450 g/1 lb cod, haddock or plaice fillets
salt and freshly ground black pepper
25/1 oz butter
4 lean bacon rashers, rind removed
Garnish
4 lemon wedges
sprigs of parsley

Wipe the fish and place the fillets in the cooking tray. Season lightly and dot with the butter. Top with the bacon rashers and cook on the hottest setting for 10 minutes. Garnish with lemon wedges and sprigs of parsley. Serve with buttered sweet corn kernels and Skewered new potatoes (see page 68).

Cheese-topped haddock

Temperature: hottest setting · Serves: 2

Lancashire cheese goes best with haddock but Caerphilly, Cheshire or mild Cheddar may be substituted.

2 (175-g/6-oz) haddock fillets
100 g/4 oz Lancashire cheese, sliced
salt and freshly ground black pepper

Place the haddock fillets in the cooking tray, top with the cheese slices and season generously. Cook on the hottest setting for 10 minutes. Serve immediately with a crisp green salad.

Spiced coley crumble

Temperature: hottest setting · Serves: 4

This is a very tasty way of serving a rather strong-flavoured but inexpensive fish.

2 tablespoons oil
1 large onion, thinly sliced
1 teaspoon ground cumin
1 teaspoon turmeric
1 clove garlic, crushed
salt and freshly ground black pepper
450 g/1 lb skinless filleted coley
100 g/4 oz mushrooms, sliced
grated rind of 1 lemon
50 g/2 oz fresh breadcrumbs
50 g/2 oz mature Cheddar cheese, grated
150 ml/$\frac{1}{4}$ pint natural yogurt

Pour the oil in the cooking tray. Sprinkle in the onion, cumin, turmeric and garlic. Season and cook on the hottest setting for 5 minutes. Cut the fish into chunks and place in the spice mixture together with the mushrooms and lemon rind. Cook for a further 3 minutes.

Mix the breadcrumbs with the cheese and season lightly. Sprinkle over the fish mixture and press down well. Cook for a further 10 minutes. Serve immediately with a bowl of natural yogurt and crisp poppadoms as accompaniments.

Grilled trout with orange and almonds

Temperature: hottest setting · Serves: 2

2 (225-g/8-oz) trout, gutted
grated rind and juice of 1 orange
25 g/1 oz flaked almonds
salt and freshly ground black pepper
50 g/2 oz butter
orange slices and watercress to garnish

Rinse and dry the trout with absorbent kitchen paper. Place in the cooking tray. Sprinkle over the orange rind and juice and the flaked almonds. Season and dot with the butter. Cook on the hottest setting for 12 minutes before serving garnished with orange slices and small bunches of watercress.

Variation

Trout is also delicious grilled with lemon and walnuts. Substitute 50 g/2 oz roughly-chopped walnuts for the almonds and the grated rind and juice of 1 lemon for the orange. Cook as above and garnish with lemon wedges.

Trout with rice and walnut stuffing

Temperature: hottest setting · Serves: 2

For a substantial meal, serve this tasty dish with a crisp salad or a selection of freshly-cooked green vegetables in season.

225 g/8 oz cooked rice (see below)
100 g/4 oz walnuts, chopped
1 small onion, finely chopped
50 g/2 oz butter
salt and freshly ground black pepper
2 tablespoons chopped parsley
2 (225-g/8-oz) trout, gutted
lemon wedges and sprigs of parsley to garnish

To cook the rice, place 75 g/3 oz easy-cook rice in the cooking tray and sprinkle with a little salt. Pour over 300 ml/ $\frac{1}{2}$ pint water and cook on the hottest setting for 15 minutes or until all the water is absorbed. Remove from the tray and keep warm. This quantity gives approximately 225 g/8 oz cooked rice.

For the stuffing, mix together the walnuts, onion and butter and spread in the cooking tray. Season generously and cook on the hottest setting for 5 minutes. Transfer to a bowl and mix in the cooked rice and parsley.

Rinse the trout and dry with absorbent kitchen paper. Place the fish in the cooking tray and divide the stuffing between them, pressing well into the body cavity. Arrange any remaining stuffing around the fish. Cook for a further 15 minutes. Transfer to a serving dish and garnish with lemon wedges and sprigs of parsley.

Sesame fish fillets with tomato mayonnaise

Temperature: hottest setting · Serves: 4

Sesame seeds add a tasty and unusual coating to white fish. Whiting particularly benefits from the extra flavour provided by the seeds.

75 g/3 oz unroasted sesame seeds
75 g/3 oz fresh breadcrumbs
salt and freshly ground black pepper
4 (100-g/4-oz) whiting fillets, skinned
50 g/2 oz plain flour
1 large egg, beaten
Tomato mayonnaise
150 ml/$\frac{1}{4}$ pint mayonnaise
2 teaspoons concentrated tomato purée
few dashes Worcestershire sauce (optional)
Garnish
1 tomato, sliced
sprigs of parsley

Mix the sesame seeds with the breadcrumbs and season generously. Coat the fish fillets first in the flour, then the beaten egg and finally in the sesame seed mixture. Press the seed mixture firmly on to the fish to form a thick, even coating. Cook the fish directly between the cooking plates on the hottest setting for 5 minutes.

Meanwhile, to make the tomato mayonnaise, mix the mayonnaise with the tomato purée and Worcestershire sauce, if used. Arrange the fish on a serving dish, garnish with tomato slices and sprigs of parsley and serve the tomato mayonnaise separately.

Baked mackerel with apple and rosemary

(Illustrated on page 34)
Temperature: hottest setting · Serves: 2

1 small cooking apple, peeled, cored and sliced
1 small onion, finely chopped
4 sprigs rosemary
salt and freshly ground black pepper
2 (225-g/8-oz) mackerel
1 tablespoon lemon juice
50 g/2 oz butter
Garnish
1 small red eating apple, sliced
fresh sprigs of rosemary

To make the stuffing, mix the sliced apple with the onion and the rosemary and season to taste. Gut the mackerel and rinse and dry on absorbent kitchen paper. Fill the cavities in the fish with the stuffing, place in the cooking tray and arrange any extra stuffing beside it. Sprinkle over a little extra seasoning and the lemon juice. Dot with the butter and cook on the hottest setting for 15 minutes.

Arrange the fish on a dish, garnish with slices of apple and small sprigs of rosemary and serve with seasonal vegetables.

Variation

Orange-stuffed mackerel Fill the fish with orange slices. Season to taste and sprinkle generously with chopped fresh herbs. Dot with butter and cook as above. Serve garnished with fresh orange slices and small sprigs of parsley.

Smoked haddock puff

Temperature: hottest setting · Serves: 4

Puff pastry is excellent when cooked in a contact grill as only a small amount of moisture is trapped in the enclosed tray. As this evaporates during cooking, the pastry puffs well and gives a crisp, light result. Be careful that the pastry dish is not too thick or the pastry will rise and touch the upper plate, thus burning slightly before the cooking process is completed.

350 g/12 oz smoked haddock fillets, skinned
100 g/4 oz mushrooms
grated rind of 1 lemon
salt and freshly ground black pepper
1 (225-g/8-oz) packet frozen puff pastry, thawed
beaten egg to glaze

Cut the fish into chunks, removing any bones. Wipe and slice the mushrooms and add to the fish, together with the lemon rind and seasoning. Mix well.

Roll out the pastry on a lightly-floured board or work surface to give a 23-cm/9-inch square and trim the edges. Place the fish mixture in the middle and dampen the edges of the pastry. Fold opposite corners to join over the filling and press the dampened edges together to form an envelope. Use any pastry trimmings to decorate the puff. Lightly press the pastry down so that it is not so high that it will come into contact with the cooking plate and burn during cooking. Carefully transfer to the tray and cook on the hottest setting for 20 minutes.

Serve hot with seasonal vegetables or a salad.

Prawns provençale

Temperature: hottest setting · Serves: 4

Serve with Melba toast as a light starter or over cooked rice (see Sweet and sour lamb chops, page 45) for a lunch or supper dish.

1 onion, sliced
1 clove garlic, crushed
3 tablespoons olive oil
salt and freshly ground black pepper
225 g/8 oz peeled cooked prawns
16 black olives, stoned
100 g/4 oz button mushrooms, halved
4 tomatoes, peeled and roughly chopped
2 tablespoons chopped parsley
grated Parmesan cheese to serve
Melba toast (see below)

Stir the onion and garlic into the olive oil and spoon into the cooking tray. Season generously and cook on the hottest setting for 5 minutes. Add the prawns, olives and mushrooms and cook for a further 10 minutes. Stir in the tomato and parsley. Serve immediately with a small bowl of grated Parmesan cheese and Melba toast.

To make the Melba toast, toast 2 medium slices of white bread directly between the cooking plates on the hottest setting for 1 minute. Quickly but carefully remove the crusts with a sharp knife and slice horizontally through each piece of bread to give two very thin pieces. Cut each piece diagonally and place in the cooking tray. Cook for a further 2-3 minutes until the toast is curled and crisp.

Melba toast may be stored for several days in an airtight container.

Bacon-coated fish cakes with yogurt sauce

(Illustrated on page 34)
Temperature: hottest setting · Serves: 8

Bacon-coated fish cakes are exceptionally tasty and make an interesting starter, a satisfying main dish served with fresh vegetables or a mixed salad, or a light supper dish.

1 (142-g/5-oz) packet instant mashed potato
450 g/1 lb cooked white fish, skinned and flaked
2 tablespoons chopped parsley
grated rind of 1 lemon
1 teaspoon anchovy essence
salt and freshly ground black pepper
1 large egg
100 g/4 oz lean bacon, rind removed and chopped
75 g/3 oz fresh breadcrumbs
50 g/2 oz plain flour
Yogurt sauce
1 tablespoon chopped mixed fresh herbs
4 tablespoons mayonnaise
150 ml/$\frac{1}{4}$ pint natural yogurt
lemon wedges and watercress to garnish

Make up the mashed potato following the instructions on the packet. Remove any bones from the cooked fish and mix into the potato together with the parsley, lemon rind and anchovy essence. Season and form into eight cakes.

Beat the egg with 2 tablespoons of water; mix the bacon with the breadcrumbs. Coat the fish cakes first in the flour and then dip in the beaten egg. Coat thoroughly in the bacon mixture and place in the greased cooking tray. Cook on the hottest setting for 5 minutes on both sides.

Meanwhile, to make the Yogurt sauce, stir the herbs into the mayonnaise, mix in the yogurt and season to taste.

Arrange the fish cakes on a serving dish and garnish with lemon wedges and small bunches of watercress. Serve immediately with the sauce poured over.

Variation

Tuna fish cakes Substitute 1 (198-g/7-oz) can of tuna for the cooked fish. Drain and flake the tuna, then continue as above.

Somerset haddock

Temperature: hottest setting · Serves: 4

50 g/2 oz butter
1 onion, chopped
1 large cooking apple
450 g/1 lb haddock fillets, skinned
salt and freshly ground black pepper
300 ml/½ pint medium-sweet cider
2 bay leaves
2 tablespoons chopped parsley

Place the butter in the cooking tray with the onion and cook on the hottest setting for 5 minutes. Meanwhile, peel, core and cut the apple into thick slices; cut the haddock into chunks and season well.

Arrange the apple with the fish in the tray. Pour over the cider, add the bay leaves and cook for a further 15 minutes.

Sprinkle with chopped parsley and serve with cooked rice (see Sweet and sour lamb chops, page 45), pasta or freshly-cooked vegetables in season.

Prawn and bacon quiche

Temperature: hottest setting · Serves: 4

Due to the direct bottom heat of a contact grill there is no need to partly cook the pastry case for a quiche before adding the filling. Use this recipe as a basic guide for cooking all your favourite quiches or for the interesting variations given below.

Shortcrust pastry
225 g/8 oz plain flour
generous pinch of salt
100 g/4 oz butter or margarine
2 tablespoons cold water
Filling
175 g/6 oz lean streaky bacon, rind removed and chopped
225 g/8 oz peeled cooked prawns
salt and freshly ground black pepper
3 eggs
250 ml/8 fl oz single cream or milk

To make the pastry, sift the flour and salt into a bowl and rub in the butter or margarine until the mixture resembles fine breadcrumbs. Mix in just enough water with a round-bladed knife to form a short dough. Roll out on a lightly-floured board or work surface and use to line the cooking tray. If the quiche is to be removed from the tray for serving, first line the tray with cooking foil so that the quiche can be lifted out easily. Alternatively, the quiche may be cut into individual portions and removed from the tray for serving.

To make the filling, sprinkle the bacon over the base of the quiche and scatter the prawns over the top. Season with plenty of freshly ground black pepper and a little salt. Lightly whisk the eggs in a bowl and gradually add the cream or milk while still whisking. Pour through a fine sieve over the prawns and cook on the hottest setting for 12-15 minutes, or until the quiche is just set and the pastry is crisp.

Variations

Prawn and mushroom quiche Substitute 100 g/4 oz sliced button mushrooms for the bacon, and cook as above.
Quiche Lorraine Substitute 100 g/4 oz thinly-sliced Gruyère cheese for the prawns and cook as above.
Cheese and onion quiche Substitute 2 finely-chopped onions and 100 g/4 oz finely-grated mature Cheddar cheese for the bacon and prawns. Cook as above.

Paella

Temperature: hottest setting · Serves: 2

100 g/4 oz uncooked chicken
100 g/4 oz streaky bacon, rind removed
1 onion, chopped
175 g/6 oz easy-cook rice
salt and freshly ground black pepper
1 teaspoon turmeric
1 clove garlic, crushed
2 tablespoons oil
450 ml/$\frac{3}{4}$ pint boiling chicken stock
225 g/8 oz peeled cooked prawns
100 g/4 oz frozen peas
1 (250-g/9-oz) can mussels in brine, drained
2 tablespoons chopped parsley
2 tomatoes, peeled and roughly chopped

Cut the chicken into bite-sized pieces; chop the bacon and place both in the cooking tray with the onion and rice. Season and add the turmeric, garlic and oil. Stir well then cook on the hottest setting for 7 minutes. Stir in the chicken stock and cook for a further 10 minutes. Add the prawns, peas and mussels and cook for another 7-10 minutes until all the stock has been absorbed. Stir in the parsley and tomato and serve immediately.

Sherried tarragon scallops

(Illustrated on front jacket)
Temperature: hottest setting · Serves: 4

1 onion, chopped
8 scallops, quartered
100 g/4 oz butter
salt and freshly ground black pepper
100 ml/4 fl oz dry sherry
rind of 1 lemon, coarsely grated
3 sprigs tarragon, chopped
450 g/1 lb potatoes, cooked
1 egg yolk

Place the onion, scallops and half the butter in the cooking tray and season generously. Cook on the hottest setting for 5 minutes. Add the sherry and cook for a further 10 minutes. Stir in the lemon rind and tarragon and cook for a further 5 minutes.

Peel the potatoes and mash in a bowl with the egg yolk and the remaining butter. Season with black pepper and, using a piping bag fitted with a large star nozzle, pipe an edge of potato around four scallop shells. Place the shells between the cooking plates with the upper plate supported in the open position if possible, or alternatively, place in the cooking tray and cook on the hottest setting for 15 minutes until lightly browned. Divide the scallop mixture between the shells, and cook for a further 2 minutes. Serve immediately.

Top: *Kidney and bacon grill (page 17)*; Below: *Individual mixed grill (page 16)*.

Scallops with bacon in cider sauce

Temperature: hottest setting · Serves: 2-4

*Serve this tasty dish with hot fresh bread for a satisfying
starter or delight your guests with a sophisticated light
meal by accompanying with a little freshly-cooked
asparagus and new potatoes.*

8 scallops
8 lean streaky bacon rashers
1 small onion, finely chopped
salt and freshly ground black pepper
25 g/1 oz butter
1 tablespoon plain flour
150 ml/$\frac{1}{4}$ pint dry cider
4 tablespoons double cream
1 tablespoon chopped parsley

Wrap each scallop in one rasher of bacon and secure with a
wooden cocktail stick. Place the scallops in the cooking tray
together with the onion and seasoning. Dot with the butter
and cook on the hottest setting for 10 minutes. Carefully
remove the cocktail sticks. Place the flour and cider in a
screw-top jar and shake vigorously until smooth. Pour over
the scallops and cook for a further 15 minutes. Stir in the
cream and parsley before serving.

Top: *Baked mackerel with apple and rosemary (page 25);*
Below: *Bacon-coated fish cakes with yogurt sauce (page 28).*

Seafood lasagne

Temperature: hottest setting · Serves: 4

Partly-cooked dried lasagne can be used straight from the packet in layers with the sauce. It is a comparatively new product which cooks very successfully, eliminating the effort involved in boiling and cooling the pasta before use. Cooked and drained lasagne can, of course, be used instead.

1 (198-g/7-oz) can tuna
1 small onion, finely chopped
1 clove garlic, crushed
1 (250-g/9-oz) can mussels in brine (optional), drained
100 g/4 oz peeled cooked prawns
1 (227-g/8-oz) can peeled tomatoes
2 tablespoons tomato purée
2 tablespoons dry sherry
salt and freshly ground black pepper
9 sheets lasagne
100 g/4 oz mature Cheddar cheese, finely grated
4 tablespoons milk

Drain the tuna and reserve the oil. Mix the onion and garlic with the reserved oil and spoon into the cooking tray. Allow to cook on the hottest setting for 5 minutes. Transfer to a bowl and mix in the flaked tuna, mussels, if used, prawns and tomatoes with the juice. Stir in the tomato purée and sherry and season well.

Place a layer of lasagne in the base of the tray, cover with a layer of the seafood sauce and continue to alternate layers of pasta and sauce, ending with a layer of lasagne. Press down well.

In a bowl, season the cheese lightly and gradually beat in the milk to form a fairly smooth, creamy mixture. Alternatively, liquidise the milk and cheese in a blender until smooth. Spread the cheese mixture over the lasagne and cook for a further 15 minutes. Serve with a crisp green salad.

MEAT DISHES

Though chops and steaks are especially good grilled, that's only the start of the meat story. Whole main courses can be cooked in minutes for a satisfying meal – piping hot casseroles, toasted kebabs, or a taste of food from other countries such as Oriental chicken or Lamb curry.

And don't forget the advantages of freezing – meat casseroles freeze well. Simply line the baking tray with cooking foil. When the casserole is cooked and has cooled, cover and freeze it in the tray, then lift out the foil parcel, seal it and pop it back into the freezer. When you want a quick meal there it is, ready for rapid defrosting and reheating once again in your contact grill.

Pork and spinach pie

Temperature: hottest setting · Serves: 4

225 g/8 oz shortcrust pastry (see Prawn and bacon quiche,
page 30)
1 onion, chopped
2 sticks celery, chopped
25 g/1 oz butter
1 (225-g/8-oz) packet frozen chopped spinach
25 g/1 oz raisins
salt and freshly ground black pepper
1 teaspoon freshly ground nutmeg
350 g/12 oz minced pork
150 ml/$\frac{1}{4}$ pint chicken stock, made from a stock cube
if necessary
beaten egg to glaze

Make the shortcrust pastry following the instructions on page
30, and chill lightly. Place the onion, celery and butter
in the cooking tray and cook on the hottest setting for 5
minutes. Defrost and thoroughly drain the spinach and add
with the raisins, seasoning and nutmeg to the onion mixture.
Mix well. Mix in the pork and press down well before
pouring over the stock.

Roll out the pastry on a lightly-floured board or work
surface to a rectangle to fit the top of the tray. Lift over the
meat mixture, trim and press the edges against the sides of
the tray. Decorate the top of the pie with any trimmings and
brush with beaten egg. Cook for 20-25 minutes until well
browned on top.

Variation

Beef and mushroom pie Substitute minced beef for the pork
and use 100 g/4 oz sliced mushrooms instead of the spinach.
Omit the raisins and nutmeg and use beef stock instead of
chicken stock. Cook as above.

Stuffed pork chops

Temperature: hottest setting · Serves: 4

25 g / 1 oz fresh breadcrumbs
50 g / 2 oz raisins, chopped
50 g / 2 oz walnuts, chopped
1 tablespoon chopped chives
1 teaspoon dried basil
grated rind of 1 orange
salt and freshly ground black pepper
4 pork loin chops
orange slices and watercress to garnish

Mix the breadcrumbs with the raisins, walnuts, herbs and orange rind. Season generously. Trim the chops and cut a slit horizontally into each to form a pocket. Press the stuffing well into the pockets. Wrap the chops loosely in cooking foil and cook directly between the cooking plates on the hottest setting for 12-15 minutes. Serve garnished with orange slices and watercress.

St Clement's spare ribs

(Illustrated on page 51)
Temperature: hottest setting · Serves: 2

450 g / 1 lb pork spare ribs
grated rind and juice of 1 orange and 1 lemon
1 small onion, finely chopped
1 teaspoon wholegrain mustard
1 tablespoon soft brown sugar
1 clove garlic, crushed
1 tablespoon tomato purée

Cut between the spare ribs and place in the cooking tray. Mix together the remaining ingredients, season and pour over the meat. Cook on the hottest setting for 30 minutes until brown.

Gammon with sweet corn and orange skewers

Temperature: hottest setting · Serves: 2

1 tablespoon runny honey
1 teaspoon olive oil
salt and freshly ground black pepper
2 gammon steaks, rind removed
Sweet corn skewers
1 corn on the cob
1 small orange
6 pickling onions
50 g/2 oz butter

Mix the honey with the oil and season lightly. Spread evenly over both sides of the gammon.

For the sweet corn skewers, remove the outer husk and silk from the corn and cut into 6 thick slices. Slice the ends off the orange and cut the remainder into three thick slices. Thread the corn, orange and onions alternately on to two skewers, dot with the butter and wrap in cooking foil, carefully sealing the ends to prevent loss of cooking juices.

Cook the corn directly between the cooking plates on the hottest setting for 20 minutes. Remove but do not unwrap. Cook the gammon directly between the plates for 4-5 minutes.

Arrange the gammon on a serving dish and top each one with a sweet corn skewer. Pour over the cooking juices and serve immediately.

Pineapple pork patties

Temperature: hottest setting · Serves: 4

450 g/1 lb minced pork
1 onion, finely chopped
1 egg
salt and freshly ground black pepper
a few drops Worcestershire sauce
4 canned pineapple rings, drained
1 tablespoon runny honey
watercress to garnish

Mix the pork with the onion and egg until thoroughly combined. Season generously and add a little Worcestershire sauce. Shape the mixture into 4 burgers and cook directly between the cooking plates on the hottest setting for 7 minutes.

Dip each pineapple ring in the honey. Place a ring on each burger and cook for a further 2 minutes until the fruit is browned. Arrange the burgers on a serving dish and garnish with small bunches of watercress.

Variations

Apple pork patties Core 1 large eating apple and cut into rings. Substitute for the pineapple and continue as above.
Orange pork patties Use thick slices of orange instead of the pineapple and continue as above.

Cumberland bacon with bananas

Temperature: hottest setting · Serves: 4

4 bacon chops or pork chops
2 tablespoons redcurrant jelly
pared rind of 1 orange, cut in thin strips
150 ml/¼ pint red wine
1 teaspoon cornflour
salt and freshly ground black pepper
2 bananas
2 tablespoons lemon juice

Place the chops in the cooking tray and cook on the hottest setting for 5 minutes.

Mix the redcurrant jelly with the orange rind and wine. Gradually stir this liquid into the cornflour to give a smooth sauce. Season lightly and pour over the chops. Cook for a further 5 minutes.

Peel and slice the bananas and dip in the lemon juice to prevent discoloration. Add to the chop mixture and cook for a further 5 minutes. Serve the chops in a dish with the sauce poured over.

This dish goes particularly well with baked or new potatoes.

Lamburgers with curried lemon sauce

Temperature: hottest setting · Serves: 4

Hamburgers and lamburgers may be served with a variety of accompaniments. Mixed salads, breads and pickles of all types can be used to ring the changes with juicy hot burgers.

salt and freshly ground black pepper
450 g/1 lb minced lean lamb
Curried lemon sauce
2 lemons, halved
1 large onion, finely chopped
2 cloves garlic, crushed
1 tablespoon grated root ginger
2 teaspoons concentrated curry paste
2 tablespoons soft brown sugar
1 tablespoon plain flour
300 ml/½ pint chicken stock, made with a stock cube
if necessary
watercress to garnish

Season the lamb to taste and shape into 4 chunky round burgers. To make the sauce, remove any pips from the lemons and finely chop both flesh and rind. Mix this with the onion, garlic and ginger and season to taste. Place in the cooking tray and cook on the hottest setting for 10 minutes. Put the remaining ingredients in a screw-top jar and shake vigorously until smooth. Add to the lemon mixture, stir well and cook for a further 15 minutes. Remove and keep the sauce warm.

Cook the lamburgers directly between the cooking plates on the hottest setting for 5-8 minutes, depending on how well cooked they are required. Serve the burgers with the hot sauce and garnish with small bunches of watercress.

Lamb cutlets with cucumber

Temperature: hottest setting · Serves: 2

4 lamb cutlets
½ cucumber, peeled and diced
1 tablespoon chopped fresh mint
salt and freshly ground black pepper
25 g/1 oz butter
4 tablespoons natural yogurt
sprigs of mint to garnish

Place the cutlets directly between the cooking plates and cook on the hottest setting for 4-5 minutes. Mix the cucumber with the mint and seasoning. Arrange the cutlets on a large piece of cooking foil and spoon the cucumber mixture around them. Dot with the butter and wrap in the cooking foil, making sure the chops are completely enclosed. Cook directly between the plates for a further 8-10 minutes.

Arrange the cutlets on the serving dish and stir the yogurt into the cooked cucumber mixture. Spoon this sauce over the cutlets and garnish with sprigs of mint. Serve immediately with new potatoes and fresh garden peas.

Sweet and sour lamb chops

(Illustrated on page 52)
Temperature: hottest setting · Serves: 4.

Cooked rice
225 g/8 oz easy-cook rice
$\frac{1}{2}$ teaspoon salt
600 ml/1 pint hot water
Sweet and sour lamb chops
25 g/1 oz butter
1 green pepper, sliced
1 onion, sliced
1 large carrot, cut into thin strips
salt and freshly ground black pepper
4 lamb chops
2 tablespoons soft brown sugar
1 tablespoon wine vinegar
2 tablespoons soy sauce
2 tablespoons tomato purée
4 tablespoons dry sherry

To cook the rice, sprinkle it in the cooking tray with the salt. Pour on the hot water and cook on the hottest setting for 20-25 minutes until all the water is absorbed. Fluff up with a fork before arranging on a serving dish. Cover with cooking foil and keep warm until the chops are cooked.

Place the butter in the cooking tray with the prepared vegetables. Season lightly and cook on the hottest setting for 5 minutes. Add the chops and cook for a further 5 minutes. Place the sugar, vinegar, soy sauce, tomato purée and sherry in a screw-top jar and shake vigorously until well combined.

Pour the sauce over the chops and continue to cook for a further 5-8 minutes. Arrange the chops and their sauce on the dish of cooked rice and serve immediately.

Caraway lamb Stroganoff

Temperature: hottest setting · Serves: 3-4

50 g/2 oz butter
1 onion, halved and thinly sliced
1 tablespoon caraway seeds
salt and freshly ground black pepper
450 g/1 lb lean boneless lamb, cut across the grain into thin
strips
1 tablespoon plain flour
150 ml/¼ pint red wine
2 teaspoons runny honey
4 tablespoons chicken stock, made with a stock cube if
necessary
150 ml/¼ pint natural yogurt
2 tablespoons chopped parsley

Place the butter in the cooking tray with the onion and caraway seeds and cook on the hottest setting for 5 minutes. Season the meat, add to the tray and cook for a further 5 minutes. Combine the flour with the wine, honey and stock in a screw-top jar and shake vigorously until well mixed. Pour over the meat and cook for a further 10 minutes.

Arrange the Stroganoff on a bed of cooked rice (see Sweet and sour lamb chops, page 45) and lightly stir in some of the yogurt. Sprinkle with the parsley and serve any remaining yogurt in a separate dish. A crisp green salad goes very well with this dish.

Variation

For a Beef Stroganoff, replace the lamb with topside of beef. Cook as above, omitting the caraway seeds.

Savoury shepherd's pie

Temperature: hottest setting · Serves: 3-4

This recipe can always be made using creamed, cooked potatoes instead of the instant mashed potato.

350 g/12 oz minced beef
1 onion, finely chopped
50 g/2 oz mushrooms, sliced
150 ml/¼ pint beef stock, made with a stock cube if necessary
2 tablespoons chopped parsley
1 (142-g/5-oz) packet instant mashed potato
100 g/4 oz Cheddar cheese, finely grated
salt and freshly ground black pepper
25 g/1 oz butter
½ teaspoon wholegrain mustard

Mix the beef with the onion and mushrooms and place in the cooking tray with the stock and parsley. Cook on the hottest setting for 5 minutes.

Make up the potato following the instructions on the packet. Stir in the cheese, seasoning and butter. Add the mustard, beat well and spread evenly over the meat in the tray. Cover loosely with a piece of cooking foil and cook for a further 5 minutes. Remove the foil and cook for 3 minutes to brown the top of the pie. Serve with seasonal vegetables.

Lamb curry with cashews

Temperature: hottest setting · Serves: 4

4 tablespoons oil
1 onion, finely chopped
3 tablespoons grated root ginger
2 cloves garlic, crushed
4 green cardamom pods
2 teaspoons turmeric
3 teaspoons ground cumin
50 g/2 oz unroasted cashew nuts
2 bay leaves
450 g/1 lb lean boneless lamb, cut into cubes
3 tablespoons peach chutney
2 tablespoons concentrated tomato purée
juice of 1 orange
1 (283-g/10-oz) can new potatoes, drained
or 450 g/1 lb cooked small new potatoes
salt and freshly ground black pepper
Cucumber raita
1 cucumber, peeled
1 tablespoon salt
150 ml/¼ pint natural yogurt

In a bowl, combine the oil, onion and spices. Add the nuts, bay leaves and the meat, toss well so the meat is thoroughly coated and place in the cooking tray. Cook on the hottest setting for 10 minutes. Stir in the chutney, tomato purée, orange juice and potatoes and season generously. Cook for a further 15 minutes, stirring to prevent sticking.

To make the cucumber raita, dice the peeled cucumber and sprinkle with the salt. Leave to stand for 20 minutes then pat dry with absorbent kitchen paper. Mix in the yogurt in a small dish. Serve the curry with the cucumber raita, cooked rice (see Sweet and sour lamb chops, page 45), Spiced aubergine and tomato (see page 63), and crisp poppadoms.

Variations

Beef curry with walnuts Substitute lean braising steak for the lamb and walnuts for the cashew nuts. Cook and serve as before, omitting the potatoes as their flavour is not strong enough to complement the beef.

Pork curry with almonds Substitute lean, boned pork for the lamb and use whole blanched almonds instead of the cashew nuts. Stir in one cored and sliced eating apple instead of the potatoes. Cook and serve as in the recipe.

Kidney casserole

Temperature: hottest setting · Serves: 3-4

1 onion, chopped
50 g/2 oz butter
salt and freshly ground black pepper
100 g/4 oz streaky bacon, rind removed and chopped
12 lamb's kidneys, cores removed
2 bay leaves
150 ml/¼ pint red vermouth
1 tablespoon concentrated tomato purée
150 ml/¼ pint canned tomato juice
100 g/4 oz small button mushrooms

Place the onion and butter in the cooking tray and cook on the hottest setting for 5 minutes. Season generously and add the bacon, kidneys and bay leaves. Add the vermouth, tomato purée and tomato juice and cook for a further 5 minutes. Lastly, add the mushrooms and cook for 10 minutes.

Serve with cooked rice (see Sweet and sour lamb chops, page 45) or Skewered new potatoes (see page 68).

Fillet steaks
with anchovy cream

Temperature: hottest setting · Serves: 4

1 (50-g/1¾-oz) can anchovy fillets, drained and chopped
100 g/4 oz cream cheese
freshly ground black pepper
2 tablespoons chopped parsley
4 fillet steaks
oil to brush
4 crisp lettuce leaves
lemon wedges to garnish

Beat the anchovies into the cream cheese. Season with a little pepper and mix in the parsley. Form into a 7.5-cm/3-inch long roll and chill thoroughly.

Brush the steaks with a little oil and cook directly between the cooking plates on the hottest setting for 2-5 minutes, depending on how well cooked the steaks are required. Arrange each steak on a leaf of lettuce, top with a slice of anchovy cream and garnish with a wedge of lemon.

Variations

The following savoury cream cheese toppings may be served instead of anchovy cream:

Lemon olive cream Finely chop 50 g/2 oz stoned black olives and beat into the cream cheese instead of the anchovies. Add the grated rind of 1 lemon and continue as above.

Blue cheese cream Mash 50 g/2 oz Danish blue cheese with the cream cheese instead of the anchovies, and continue as above.

Spiced orange cream Beat 1 teaspoon freshly-grated nutmeg and the grated rind of 1 orange into the cream cheese instead of the anchovies and continue as above.

St Clement's spare ribs with Aubergine and leek risotto (pages 39 and 62).

Steak au marron

Temperature: hottest setting · Serves: 2

50 g/2 oz ham, finely chopped
5 tablespoons unsweetened chestnut purée
1 tablespoon brandy
salt and freshly ground black pepper
2 spring onions, finely chopped
1 (450-g/1-lb) slice rump steak
oil to brush
Celery and apple salad
6 sticks celery, chopped
2 eating apples, cored and sliced
1 bunch watercress, trimmed and chopped
3 tablespoons lemon juice
150 ml/¼ pint double cream
2 teaspoons runny honey
2 teaspoons chopped mixed fresh herbs
croûtes (optional)
watercress to garnish

Mix the ham with the chestnut purée, brandy, seasoning and spring onion. Trim the steak and cut a horizontal slit with a sharp knife to form a neat pocket. Take care not to cut right through the steak. Press the chestnut mixture well into the pocket and brush the steak with a little oil. Cook directly between the cooking plates on the hottest setting for 5-6 minutes.

To make the celery and apple salad, mix the celery and apple with the chopped watercress and season to taste. Stir the lemon juice into the cream, then mix in the honey and herbs. Season to taste and pour over the celery mixture. Toss well just before serving.

Serve the steak on a large platter surrounded by the salad. Top with 4 large croûtes, if liked (see Smoked mackerel cream, page 81) and garnish with small bunches of water-cress.

Clockwise: *Sweet and sour lamb chops (page 45); Courgette quiche (page 65); Hamburgers (page 54).*

Hamburgers

(Illustrated on page 52)
Temperature: hottest setting · Serves: 4

salt and freshly ground black pepper
450 g/1 lb lean minced beef
4 baps or soft rolls
4 crisp lettuce leaves
1 small onion, sliced into rings
2 tomatoes, sliced
selection of pickles (optional)

Season the beef to taste and shape into 4 burgers. Cook directly between the cooking plates on the hottest setting for 4-8 minutes, depending on how well cooked they are required.

Split the baps or rolls in half and place a lettuce leaf on each base. Arrange the onion rings, tomato and choice of pickles, if used, on top of the cooked burger before placing the burger on the bap or roll. Top with the other half of the bap or roll. Serve immediately. Alternatively, sandwich the burger in the bun and serve the salad garnishes separately.

Variations

Blue cheese burgers Cream 100 g/4 oz Danish blue cheese with 50 g/2 oz full fat soft cream cheese until smooth. Arrange the cooked burgers on a lettuce leaf and top with the cheese cream. Serve immediately.

Provençal burgers Cook the burgers as above. To make a Provençal sauce, peel and chop 8 tomatoes and mix with 1 finely-chopped onion and 100 g/4 oz halved, stoned black olives. Season to taste and cook in the cooking tray on the hottest setting for 5 minutes. Arrange the cooked burgers on a serving dish and top with this sauce. Serve with cooked rice (see Sweet and sour lamb chops, page 45) or baked potatoes.

Liver with pimiento and prunes

Temperature: hottest setting · Serves: 4

350 g/12 oz lamb's liver, sliced
1 onion, thinly sliced
1 (190-g/6¾-oz) can pimientos, drained and sliced
1 (213-g/7½-oz) can prunes in syrup, drained and stoned
25 g/1 oz butter
salt and freshly ground black pepper
6 tablespoons port

Arrange the liver, onion and pimientos in the cooking tray together with the prunes. Dot with the butter and season generously. Cook on the hottest setting for 10 minutes then add the port and cook for a further 10 minutes. Serve immediately with cooked rice (see Sweet and sour lamb chops, page 45).

Devilled drumsticks

Temperature: hottest setting · Serves: 2

1 tablespoon soft brown sugar
1 tablespoon concentrated tomato purée
1 teaspoon wholegrain mustard
salt and freshly ground black pepper
dash of Worcestershire sauce
4 chicken drumsticks

In a bowl, mix together the sugar, tomato purée, mustard and seasoning. Make 2 deep incisions with a sharp knife into each drumstick and spread with all the sauce. Wrap the chicken in cooking foil and cook directly between the cooking plates on the hottest setting for 20 minutes.
Serve with hot French bread and a mixed salad.

Stuffed chicken breasts

Temperature: hottest setting · Serves: 4

1 (227-g/8-oz) can apricot halves, drained
50 g/2 oz fresh breadcrumbs
1 bunch spring onions, trimmed and chopped
grated rind of 1 orange
1 tablespoon chopped mixed fresh herbs
salt and freshly ground black pepper
4 boneless chicken breasts
8 lean streaky bacon rashers, rind removed

Chop the apricots and mix with the breadcrumbs, spring onion, orange rind, fresh herbs and seasoning. Make a slit with a sharp knife into each chicken breast to form a pocket. Divide the stuffing between the chicken breasts and press well into the pocket. Wrap each breast in two bacon rashers and secure with a wooden cocktail stick. Loosely wrap the chicken in cooking foil and cook directly between the cooking plates on the hottest setting for 12-15 minutes. Remove the cocktail sticks and serve the chicken breasts with a crisp green salad.

Oriental chicken

Temperature: hottest setting · Serves: 2

To give oriental dishes an authentic flavour, it is important to use sesame oil in cooking. This oil imparts a rich, nutty flavour to the food but can overpower a dish when used in excessive quantities. It is also a useful ingredient to remember when mixing salad dressings. Vegetable oil may be substituted in most cases.

1 red pepper, deseeded and cut into thin strips
15 g/½ oz fresh root ginger, grated
350 g/12 oz uncooked chicken, shredded
1 clove garlic, crushed
2 tablespoons sesame or vegetable oil
1 (227-g/8-oz) can water chestnuts, drained
1 (227-g/8-oz) can bamboo shoots, drained
2 teaspoons cornflour
2 tablespoons soy sauce
4 tablespoons dry sherry
4 tablespoons chicken stock, made with a stock cube if necessary
salt and freshly ground black pepper

Place the red pepper, ginger, chicken and garlic in the cooking tray with the oil and cook on the hottest setting for 5 minutes.

Meanwhile, halve the water chestnuts and slice the bamboo shoots. Place the remaining ingredients in a screw-top jar and shake vigorously until well combined. Season to taste. Add the water chestnuts and bamboo shoots to the tray and mix well. Pour over the sauce and cook for 8 minutes. Serve on a bed of cooked rice (see Sweet and sour lamb chops, page 45).

Chicken in wine sauce

(Illustrated on page 85)
Temperature: hottest setting · Serves: 4

50 g/2 oz butter
1 onion, sliced
2 tablespoons plain flour
1 chicken stock cube
300 ml/½ pint red or white wine
4 chicken breasts, boned
100 g/4 oz button mushrooms, sliced
3 tablespoons double cream
2 tablespoons chopped parsley

Place the butter and onion in the cooking tray and cook on the hottest setting for 5 minutes. Place the flour, the crumbled stock cube and wine in a screw-top jar and shake vigorously until smooth and well blended. Pour into the tray and cook for a further 5 minutes.

Remove the tray. Cook the chicken directly between the cooking plates on the hottest setting for 3 minutes or until brown. Add the chicken to the sauce in the tray and cook for a further 5 minutes. Lastly, add the mushrooms and stir in the cream. Cook for 5 minutes. Stir in the parsley before serving with cooked rice (see Sweet and sour lamb chops, page 45).

Crunchy chicken with orange mayonnaise

Temperature: hottest setting · Serves: 2

2 chicken breasts, boned
50 g/2 oz fresh breadcrumbs
1 teaspoon dried mixed herbs
2 tablespoons plain flour
salt and freshly ground black pepper
1 egg, lightly beaten
Orange mayonnaise
150 ml/¼ pint mayonnaise
grated rind of 1 orange and juice of ½ orange
1 clove garlic, crushed
4 spring onions, chopped

Remove the skin from the chicken breasts and place each one between two sheets of greaseproof paper. Beat with a rolling pin until thin. Mix the breadcrumbs with the dried herbs. Coat the chicken in the flour and seasoning then in the egg and finally in the breadcrumbs and mixed herbs. Cook directly between the cooking plates on the hottest setting for 8 minutes.

To make the orange mayonnaise, mix all the remaining ingredients together and serve separately in a small dish. Serve the chicken with a salad of your choice and plain boiled new potatoes or a cold rice or pasta salad.

Variations

This dish may be made with turkey breasts or veal fillets, beaten out and prepared as above. Serve the turkey with the orange mayonnaise; serve the veal with a lemon mayonnaise by substituting lemon for the orange.

Chestnut turkey kebabs

Temperature: hottest setting · Serves: 2-4

These unusual kebabs may be served as a first course or accompanied by a selection of salads as a main dish.

6 tablespoons unsweetened chestnut purée
1 tablespoon brandy
salt and freshly ground black pepper
6 lean streaky bacon rashers, halved
3 small onions, quartered
12 bay leaves
450 g/1 lb uncooked turkey, cubed
oil for brushing

Mix the chestnut purée with the brandy and seasoning. Spread the chestnut mixture over each piece of bacon and roll up. Thread the bacon rolls alternately with the onions, bay leaves and turkey cubes on to 4 skewers. Brush with a little oil and cook directly between the cooking plates on the hottest setting for 7-10 minutes. Serve immediately.

Variation

(Illustrated on front jacket)

For an equally delicious kebab to serve 4, use chicken instead of turkey. Thread the meat alternately on to 8 skewers with bay leaves, 8 bacon rashers, rinds removed and rolled, 8 pickling onions and 4 small tomatoes, halved. Cook as above. Serve 2 skewers per person.

VEGETABLES

Crisp and fresh or straight from the freezer, wherever your vegetables come from they'll emerge from your contact grill with flavour and texture intact. No more soggy cabbage – rapid cooking in high heat with little moisture added is the best route to success.

The varied vegetable dishes that follow can be served as accompaniments or will even provide a main course. Potatoes, too, can be prepared in different ways, and those oven-ready chips, for instance, can be baked from frozen in a matter of minutes.

Be adventurous – for a vegetarian meal serve the delicious Aubergine and leek risotto, or try the Courgettes with almonds and bacon for a tasty starter served with hot crusty bread.

Aubergine and leek risotto

(Illustrated on page 51)
Temperature: hottest setting · Serves: 2

This risotto is ideal as a side dish for a dinner or supper party or as a tasty vegetarian meal.

2 tablespoons oil
50 g/2 oz butter
100 g/4 oz easy-cook rice
300 ml/$\frac{1}{2}$ pint chicken stock or 2 tablespoons yeast extract
dissolved in 300 ml/$\frac{1}{2}$ pint hot water
1 small aubergine, diced
1 leek, trimmed and sliced
2 tomatoes, peeled
salt and freshly ground black pepper
Croûtons
4 thin slices white bread
50 g/2 oz butter
2 tablespoons chopped parsley

Place the oil, butter and rice in the cooking tray and cook on the hottest setting for 5 minutes. Add the stock or yeast extract and hot water, the aubergine and leek and cook for a further 15 minutes. Stir in the tomatoes and cook for a further 5 minutes. Taste and adjust the seasoning.

To make the croûtons, remove the crusts from the bread and butter each slice very lightly on both sides. Cook directly between the cooking plates on the hottest setting for 2-3 minutes then cut into small squares or triangles. Mix the croûtons with the parsley and sprinkle over the risotto before serving.

Spiced aubergine with tomatoes

Temperature: hottest setting · Serves: 2

This dish makes an unusual starter, a main meal accompaniment or, alternatively, it makes a good vegetarian dish when served with cooked brown rice.

1 aubergine, chopped
2 tablespoons salt
6 tablespoons olive oil
2 cloves garlic, crushed
2 tablespoons grated root ginger
100 g/4 oz cashew nuts
1 onion, thinly sliced
4 tomatoes, peeled and quartered
2 teaspoons garam masala (see note)
salt and freshly ground black pepper

Place the aubergine in a strainer and sprinkle over the salt. Allow to stand for 20 minutes then rinse and pat dry with absorbent kitchen paper.

Place the olive oil, garlic, ginger and nuts in the cooking tray and cook on the hottest setting for 5 minutes. Add the onion, aubergine and tomato quarters and sprinkle over the garam masala. Mix well and cook for 10 minutes. Taste and adjust the seasoning before serving.

Note Garam masala is a mixture of spices, usually added towards the end of the cooking time. It normally consists of cumin and coriander seeds, bay leaves, peppercorns, cloves, cinnamon and mace, all lightly roasted together to accentuate the flavours and then ground to a fine powder. It is widely available in packets or cans. Buy small cans if your use is limited, as once opened, the flavour will deteriorate.

Ratatouille

Temperature: hottest setting · Serves: 2

1 small aubergine, diced
1 tablespoon salt
6 tablespoons olive oil
1 onion, halved and sliced
1 large clove garlic, crushed
salt and freshly ground black pepper
1 small green pepper, halved, deseeded and sliced
1 courgette, thinly sliced
2 tomatoes, peeled and chopped
2 tablespoons chopped parsley

Place the aubergine in a strainer and sprinkle over the salt. Leave to stand for 20 minutes then rinse and pat dry with absorbent kitchen paper.

Pour the oil in the cooking tray and add the onion, garlic and seasoning. Add the green pepper and the courgette and cook on the hottest setting for 15 minutes. Stir in the tomato and parsley just before serving.

Courgettes with almonds and bacon

Temperature: hottest setting · Serves: 4

4 courgettes, trimmed
100 g/4 oz blanched almonds
175 g/6 oz smoked streaky bacon, rind removed and chopped
salt and freshly ground black pepper

Place the courgettes whole in the cooking tray. Sprinkle over the almonds, bacon and seasoning. Cook on the hottest setting for 10 minutes and serve immediately.

Courgette quiche

(Illustrated on page 52)
Temperature: hottest setting · Serves: 4-6

450 g/1 lb courgettes, trimmed, thinly peeled and sliced
1 tablespoon salt
225 g/8 oz shortcrust pastry (see Prawn and bacon quiche,
page 30)
1 tablespoon chopped dill
50 g/2 oz Cheddar cheese, grated
freshly grated nutmeg
3 eggs
300 ml/½ pint milk

Place the courgettes in a strainer, sprinkle with the salt and allow to stand for 20-30 minutes. Rinse and pat dry thoroughly with absorbent kitchen paper. Roll out the pastry on a lightly-floured board or work surface and use to line the cooking tray. Arrange the courgettes in the pastry case, sprinkle over the dill and cheese and season with nutmeg. Beat the eggs with the milk, pour into the pastry shell and cook on the hottest setting for 20 minutes. Serve hot or cold.

Variations

Asparagus quiche Substitute 225 g/8 oz cooked, canned or frozen and thawed asparagus for the courgettes. Continue as above.
Spinach quiche Substitute 225 g/8 oz cooked, chopped spinach for the courgettes and continue as above.

Asparagus mille feuilles

Temperature: hottest setting · Serves: 4-6

Serve this mille feuilles as a starter, light lunch or part of a buffet supper.

1 (370-g/13-oz) packet frozen puff pastry, thawed
1 small onion, finely chopped
100 g/4 oz lean streaky bacon, rind removed and finely chopped
2 tablespoons plain flour
300 ml/½ pint milk
25 g/1 oz butter
salt and freshly ground black pepper
1 (340-g/12-oz) can asparagus spears, drained

Roll out the pastry on a lightly-floured board or work surface to give an 18 x 40-cm/7 x 16-inch rectangle. Cut in half to give two pieces measuring 18 x 20 cm/7 x 8 inches. Cook the pastry, one sheet at a time, in the cooking tray on the hottest setting for 12-15 minutes each. Remove to cool on a wire rack.

Place the onion and bacon in the tray and cook for 5 minutes. Put the flour, milk and butter in a screw-top jar and shake vigorously until smooth. Season to taste and pour over the bacon mixture. Stir well and cook for 3 minutes. Add the asparagus, stir again and cook for a further 5 minutes. Place one sheet of pastry on a serving dish, top with the sauce and place the remaining pastry on top. Serve immediately.

Stuffed cabbage leaves

Temperature: hottest setting · Serves: 4

175 g/6 oz cooked chicken, chopped
225 g/8 oz Frankfurter sausages, chopped
1 small cooking apple, peeled and cored
2 tablespoons chopped chives
salt and freshly ground black pepper
100 g/4 oz fresh breadcrumbs
8 large green cabbage leaves
Sauce
3 tablespoons tomato purée
1 chicken stock cube
1 tablespoon plain flour
1 tablespoon soft brown sugar
450 ml/$\frac{3}{4}$ pint red wine

In a bowl mix the chicken with the Frankfurters. Grate the apple and add to the chicken mixture together with the chives, seasoning and breadcrumbs. Mix well.

Wash the cabbage leaves, place in a large bowl and cover with boiling water. Leave to stand for 5 minutes, then drain and dry on absorbent kitchen paper. Place a little of the stuffing on each leaf and carefully fold up to form a neat parcel. Arrange the cabbage parcels in the cooking tray.

To make the sauce, put all the remaining ingredients together in a screw-top jar and shake vigorously until smooth. Pour the sauce over the cabbage, cover with cooking foil and cook on the hottest setting for 15 minutes. Serve immediately with cooked rice (see Sweet and sour lamb chops, page 45).

Skewered new potatoes

Temperature: hottest setting · Serves: 2

These make an unusual but simple accompaniment that complements grilled meat or fish.

10 even-sized, small new potatoes, scrubbed
vegetable oil
mixed herb butter

Thread the potatoes on to 2 skewers and brush on all sides with a little oil. Wrap loosely in cooking foil, place in the cooking tray and cook on the hottest setting for 15 minutes. Remove the foil and cook for a further 10-15 minutes. Serve immediately with Mixed herb butter (see page 117).

Rösti

Temperature: hottest setting · Serves: 4

1 kg/2 lb potatoes, peeled and sliced
1 onion, halved and sliced
175 g/6 oz streaky bacon, rind removed and chopped
salt and freshly ground black pepper
3 tablespoons water
50 g/2 oz butter
75 g/3 oz Cheddar cheese, grated

In the cooking tray, layer the potatoes alternately with the onion and bacon, seasoning each layer well. Sprinkle with the water and dot with the butter. Cover with cooking foil and cook on the hottest setting for 30 minutes.

Remove the foil, sprinkle with the cheese and press down well. Cook for a further 5 minutes, uncovered. Serve immediately as a light supper dish or as an accompaniment to grilled meat.

Duchesse potatoes

Temperature: hottest setting · Serves: 4

1 (142-g/5-oz) packet instant mashed potato or
450 g/1 lb cooked potatoes, creamed
1 egg yolk
25 g/1 oz butter
salt and freshly ground white pepper

Grease the cooking tray. Make up the mashed potato following the instructions on the packet and beat in the egg yolk,
butter and seasoning. Place in a piping bag fitted with a large
star nozzle and pipe swirls of potato into the cooking tray.
Cook on the hottest setting for 25 minutes until golden brown.

Variation

The potato may also be piped into 'nests' and cooked in the
same way. To serve, transfer carefully on to a dish or
individual plates. Fill as required, for example, Pork and
spinach pie filling (see page 38).

Spicy spinach and rice cakes

Temperature: hottest setting · Serves: 4

100 g/4 oz easy-cook rice
generous pinch of salt
150 ml/$\frac{1}{4}$ pint water
1 (227-g/8-oz) packet frozen chopped spinach, thawed and
thoroughly drained
$\frac{1}{2}$ teaspoon mixed spice
salt and freshly ground black pepper
1 tablespoon plain flour
1 small egg, lightly beaten
50 g/2 oz butter

Cook the rice with the salt and water following the instructions for the cooked rice in Sweet and sour lamb chops on page 45. Mix the spinach, spice, seasoning and flour into the cooked rice, bind with the beaten egg and leave until cold.

Shape the rice mixture into 4 cakes and place in the cooking tray. Dot with the butter and cook on the hottest setting for 15 minutes, turning the cakes once during cooking. Serve immediately.

70

SUPPER DISHES

You can save on the washing up by using your contact grill to provide light lunches, supper and picnic fare – no messy saucepans or casseroles needed and there'll be plenty of time left over to spend on more important things. Pizzas, pasties, moussaka and many other dishes are well within the capacity of your versatile grill, or you could try the Traditional Spanish omelette or the Sausage and chick pea bake suggested here.

All the recipes in this chapter are valuable standbys for a snatched lunch or a hurried supper when you've been working late. And the recipe given for Toad in the hole could easily be adapted to make a rapid Yorkshire pudding if you find at the last moment you have forgotten to provide one with the Sunday joint!

Salami pizza

Temperature: hottest setting · Serves: 4

225 g/8 oz self-raising flour
pinch of salt
50 g/2 oz butter
150 ml/¼ pint milk
2 tablespoons concentrated tomato purée
1 large onion, finely chopped
salt and freshly ground black pepper
1 tablespoon dried oregano or marjoram
100 g/4 oz full fat soft cheese, diced
175 g/6 oz salami, thinly sliced
12 stuffed green olives, sliced
50 g/2 oz Cheddar cheese, grated

Sift the flour and salt into a bowl. Rub in the butter until the mixture resembles fine breadcrumbs. Stir in the milk to form a soft dough. Knead lightly on a well-floured board or work surface, then roll out to line the greased cooking tray.

Mix the tomato purée with the onion, seasoning and oregano or marjoram. Spread over the pastry base and dot with the soft cheese. Arrange the salami and olives on top and sprinkle over the grated Cheddar cheese. Cook on the hottest setting for 12 minutes. Serve hot or cold.

Variation

Lemon sardine pizza Mix 1 (120-g/4¼-oz) can drained sardines in oil and the grated rind of 2 lemons with the tomato purée mixture. Season and spread over the pastry base. Omit the salami and stuffed olives. Top the sardine mixture with the soft cheese and grated Cheddar cheese. Press down well and arrange a lattice of 2 (56-g/2-oz) cans of drained anchovy fillets and 100 g/4 oz stoned sliced black olives on top. Cook as above.

Pitta bread pizzas

Temperature: hottest setting · Serves: 2

1 onion, finely chopped
1 tablespoon dried basil
salt and freshly ground black pepper
2 pitta breads
50 g/2 oz mushrooms, sliced
2 large tomatoes, sliced
100 g/4 oz cheese, thinly sliced
1 (56-g/2-oz) can anchovy fillets, drained
8-10 stoned black olives, sliced

Mix the onion with the basil and season generously. Spread over the pitta bread. Layer the mushrooms and tomatoes on the bread and top with the cheese. Place in the cooking tray and cook on the hottest setting for 8-10 minutes. Arrange the anchovy fillets and olives on top and cook for a further 2 minutes. Serve immediately.

Variation

Cucumber and ham pizzas Spread each pitta bread with 1 tablespoon tomato purée. Sprinkle over 1 finely-chopped onion and $\frac{1}{2}$ lightly-peeled and chopped cucumber. Season generously. Top with 4 slices cooked ham, 100 g/4 oz sliced cheese and cook as above. Top with 2 sliced tomatoes and 8-10 halved, stoned black olives and cook for a further 2 minutes. Serve immediately.

Stuffed sausage

Temperature: hottest setting · Serves: 4

100 g/4 oz button mushrooms
100 g/4 oz full fat soft cheese
1 tablespoon redcurrant jelly
50 g/2 oz breadcrumbs
1 tablespoon chopped mixed fresh herbs, or
1 teaspoon mixed dried herbs
3 spring onions, chopped
salt and freshly ground black pepper
1 (340-g/12-oz) smoked Dutch sausage

Wipe, trim and chop the mushrooms. Place in a bowl and mix with the cheese, redcurrant jelly, breadcrumbs, herbs and onion, and season generously. Cut a slit along the length of the sausage and carefully open out. Spoon the stuffing into the slit, and secure the stuffed sausage by wrapping completely in cooking foil. Place in the cooking tray and cook on the hottest setting for 5 minutes. Serve immediately with a salad and new potatoes.

Variation

Stuffed sausage with apple and bacon Substitute 1 medium cooking apple, peeled and grated, for the mushrooms, and add 225 g/8 oz finely-chopped bacon, 2 teaspoons wholegrain mustard and the grated rind of 1 lemon to the mixture. Omit the redcurrant jelly, herbs and spring onions. Cook as above.

Toad in the hole

Temperature: hottest setting · Serves: 2

The contact grill cooks the lightest of batters in a very short time. Use double the quantity of batter from this recipe to make a delicious Yorkshire pudding in only a fraction of the time it would normally take.

4 thick pork sausages
Batter
50 g/2 oz plain flour
pinch of salt
1 egg
150 ml/¼ pint milk

Place the sausages in the greased cooking tray. To make the batter, sift the flour and salt into a bowl and gradually beat in the egg and milk to give a light, smooth batter. Carefully pour the batter around the sausages and cook on the hottest setting for 10 minutes. Serve immediately

Variation

Porker in the grass Chop 225 g/8 oz cooked ham into large chunks and use instead of the sausages. Add 1 very finely-chopped small onion and 1 tablespoon chopped fresh herbs to the batter and cook as above.

Glamorgan sausages

Temperature: hottest setting · Serves: 4

This mixture may also be shaped into small cakes instead of sausages. These are a firm favourite with children.

175 g/6 oz mature Cheddar cheese
100 g/4 oz fresh breadcrumbs
1 teaspoon wholegrain mustard
2 tablespoons milk
salt and freshly ground black pepper
1 egg, lightly beaten
75 g/3 oz dry white breadcrumbs
2 tablespoons oil

Mix the cheese in a bowl with the breadcrumbs, mustard and milk and season generously. Divide the mixture into quarters and shape each into a sausage. Dip each sausage in the egg and coat with the dry breadcrumbs. Heat the oil in the cooking tray on the hottest setting for 30 seconds. Add the sausages and cook for 10 minutes, turning once during cooking. Serve warm.

Variations

Cheese and ham sausages Add 100 g/4 oz finely-chopped ham to the mixture. Coat and cook as above.
Herby onion cheese cakes Add 2 tablespoons chopped mixed fresh herbs and 1 finely-chopped onion to the basic mixture. Shape into round cakes instead of sausages. Coat and cook as above.

Frankfurter and apple casserole

Temperature: hottest setting · Serves: 4

25 g/1 oz butter
1 (340-g/12-oz) packet Frankfurter sausages
8 lean streaky bacon rashers, rind removed
1 onion, sliced
1 eating apple, cored and thickly sliced
2 teaspoons cornflour
$\frac{1}{2}$ chicken stock cube
300 ml/$\frac{1}{2}$ pint dry ginger ale
salt and freshly ground black pepper

Place the butter and Frankfurters in the cooking tray. Roll up the bacon rashers, secure with a wooden cocktail stick and add to the tray with the onion. Cook on the hottest setting for 5 minutes. Remove the cocktail sticks from the bacon and add the sliced apple. Place the cornflour, the crumbled stock cube and ginger ale in a screw-top jar and shake vigorously until smooth. Pour into the cooking tray, season lightly and cook for 10 minutes. Serve with cooked rice (see Sweet and sour lamb chops, page 45) or baked potatoes.

Sausage and chick pea bake

Temperature: hottest setting · Serves: 2

This dish is a delicious light meal in itself. Canned chick peas are quick to use and absorb flavours from the other ingredients in the recipe.

225 g/8 oz pork sausages
1 onion, sliced
2 cloves garlic, crushed
1 (425-g/15-oz) can chick peas, drained
100 g/4 oz button mushrooms, sliced
salt and freshly ground black pepper
300 ml/½ pint chicken stock, made with a stock cube if necessary
1 tablespoon concentrated tomato purée
2 tomatoes, peeled and roughly chopped
2 tablespoons chopped parsley

Place the sausages in the cooking tray with the onion and garlic. Cook on the hottest setting for 5 minutes. Add the chick peas and mushrooms and season lightly. Cook for a further 3 minutes. Mix the stock with the tomato purée, add to the cooking tray and cook for a further 10 minutes. Stir in the tomato and parsley before serving.

Pork and almond pasties

Temperature: hottest setting · Makes: 4

These little pasties are ideal served hot but are also good for packed lunches and picnics.

225 g/8 oz shortcrust pastry (see Prawn and bacon quiche, page 30)
225 g/8 oz minced pork
1 small onion, finely chopped
100 g/4 oz blanched almonds, chopped
$\frac{1}{2}$ teaspoon mixed spice
salt and freshly ground black pepper
beaten egg to glaze

Make the pastry dough, following the recipe instructions. Divide into 4 portions and roll out each portion on a lightly-floured board or work surface into a 15-cm/6-inch circle. Mix the remaining ingredients, except the egg, together in a bowl and divide between the pastry circles. Dampen the pastry edges, fold them over the filling and press the edges together gently to form a semi-circular pasty. Flatten slightly and place in the cooking tray. Brush with beaten egg and cook on the hottest setting for 20 minutes. Serve hot or cold.

Variations

Chicken and ham pasties Mix 450 g/1 lb chopped uncooked chicken with 100 g/4 oz diced cooked ham and 1 bunch spring onions, chopped. Season generously and use to fill the pasties. Cook as above.

Beefy bean pasties Mix 225 g/8 oz minced beef with 1 finely-chopped onion, 1 crumbled beef stock cube and 1 (142-g/5-oz) can baked beans. Use to fill the pasties and cook as above. This is a tasty snack for hungry children!

Quick and easy moussaka

Temperature: hottest setting · Serves: 2

1 aubergine, chopped
2 teaspoons salt
225 g/8 oz minced lamb
1 small onion, finely chopped
1 clove garlic, crushed
salt and freshly ground black pepper
2 large tomatoes, peeled and chopped
150 g/5 oz Cheddar cheese, finely grated
1 egg, lightly beaten
4 tablespoons milk
a little freshly grated nutmeg
2 tablespoons chopped parsley

Place the chopped aubergine in a strainer, sprinkle over the salt and leave to stand and drain for 20 minutes. Mix the lamb in a bowl with the onion and garlic and season generously. Place in the cooking tray and cook on the hottest setting for 5 minutes. Rinse and dry the aubergine on absorbent kitchen paper and mix with the tomatoes. Press evenly over the meat. Mix 100 g/4 oz of the cheese with the egg and milk, season lightly and pour over the aubergine. Sprinkle over the nutmeg, top with the remaining grated cheese and cook for a further 10 minutes. Sprinkle with chopped parsley before serving.

Smoked mackerel cream

Temperature: hottest setting · Serves: 2

2 tablespoons plain flour
25 g/1 oz butter
300 ml/½ pint milk
4 teaspoons creamed horseradish
3 smoked mackerel fillets, skinned
salt and freshly ground black pepper
Croûtes
75 g/3 oz butter
4 thin slices bread
Garnish
3 tablespoons chopped parsley
grated rind of 2 lemons

Put the flour, butter and milk in a screw-top jar and shake vigorously until smooth. Pour into the cooking tray and cook on the hottest setting for 3 minutes. Stir in the horseradish. Remove any bones from the fish and separate the flesh into chunks. Add to the sauce and cook for a further 3 minutes. Adjust the seasoning if necessary. Place in a serving dish and keep warm.

To make the croûtes, butter both sides of the bread generously. Place directly between the cooking plates and cook on the hottest setting for 1 minute. Turn the slices around so that the lines from the cooking plates mark the bread in the opposite direction and cook for a further 1-2 minutes. Working quickly, remove the crusts and cut each slice diagonally into 4 triangles.

Arrange the croûtes around the creamed mackerel, serving any spare ones in a separate dish. Garnish with alternate lines of chopped parsley and grated lemon rind. Serve immediately with cooked rice (see Sweet and sour lamb chops, page 45).

Savoury creamed rice

Temperature: hottest setting · Serves: 2

This recipe is a good way of using up left-over cooked meats or small quantities of vegetables. For example, chopped celery, peppers or carrots may be added with the onion; diced cooked chicken, pork or ham may be added with the rice.

100 g/4 oz lean bacon, rind removed and chopped
1 onion, chopped
25 g/1 oz butter
100 g/4 oz easy-cook rice
300 ml/½ pint chicken stock, made with a stock cube if necessary
salt and freshly ground black pepper
100 g/4 oz button mushrooms, sliced
1 (198-g/7-oz) can sweet corn kernels, drained
150 ml/¼ pint single cream
Garnish
2 tablespoons chopped parsley
paprika pepper

Spread the bacon in the cooking tray with the onion and butter and cook on the hottest setting for 5 minutes. Add the rice and chicken stock and season lightly. Cook for a further 10 minutes. Finally, stir in the mushrooms, sweet corn and cream and cook for 5 minutes. Transfer to a serving dish and garnish with the chopped parsley and paprika. Serve hot with a crisp green salad.

Chicken and ham roulade

Temperature: hottest setting · Serves: 4

Chicken and ham roulade, served with a crisp green salad, makes an elegant lunch dish. This sophisticated recipe emphasises the versatility of the contact grill for the more ambitious cook.

3 eggs, separated
175 g/6 oz cooked ham, finely chopped
4 tablespoons double cream
salt and freshly ground black pepper
50 g/2 oz plain flour, sifted
450 g/1 lb cooked chicken, finely chopped
4 spring onions, chopped
150 ml/¼ pint mayonnaise
1 teaspoon wholegrain mustard
1 small clove garlic, crushed
2 tablespoons double cream
tomato and cucumber slices to garnish

Line the cooking tray with greaseproof paper and grease thoroughly. Beat the egg yolks in a bowl with the ham, double cream and seasoning. Fold in the flour. Whisk the egg whites until stiff and fold into the ham mixture. Turn the mixture into the cooking tray, spread evenly and cook on the hottest setting for 5 minutes.

Meanwhile, mix the chicken with the spring onion, mayonnaise, mustard, garlic and cream until thoroughly combined. Turn out the roulade on to greaseproof paper, trim the edges and spread with the chicken mixture. Roll up tightly and serve garnished with sliced tomatoes and cucumber.

Variation

Chicken and prawn roulade Substitute 50 g/2 oz grated cheese mixed with the grated rind of 1 lemon for the ham. Use 225 g/8 oz cooked chicken and 225 g/8 oz peeled cooked prawns in the filling. Continue as above.

Traditional Spanish omelette

Temperature: hottest setting · Serves: 2

50 g/2 oz butter
1 large onion, chopped
350 g/12 oz cooked potatoes, peeled and diced
4 large eggs
4 tablespoons milk
salt and freshly ground black pepper

Put the butter in the cooking tray with the onion and cook on the hottest setting for 5 minutes. Spread the potato evenly over the tray. Whisk the eggs with the milk and season generously. Pour over the potato mixture and cook for a further 8-10 minutes. Serve immediately.

Variations

Mixed vegetable omelette Use half the quantity of cooked potatoes. Add 1 small deseeded and chopped red pepper and green pepper and 1 diced carrot with the onions. Continue as above.

Bacon and sweet corn omelette Add 100 g/4 oz chopped lean bacon, rind removed, with the onion. Use half the quantity of cooked potatoes and add 1 (178-g/7-oz) can drained sweet corn kernels. Continue as above.

Herby mushroom omelette Add 225 g/8 oz very small button mushrooms instead of the potatoes and stir 1 tablespoon chopped mixed fresh herbs into the eggs. Continue as above.

Top: *Chicken in wine sauce (page 58);* Below: *Devilled drumsticks (page 55);*
Overleaf: Top: *Summer lemon slices (page 91);* Centre: *Baked apples with raisin and orange sauce (page 90);* Below: *Gingered rhubarb crumble (page 89).*

PUDDINGS & DESSERTS

For many of us the dessert course is the best part of a meal, and it can certainly be the most tempting. No need to cook in advance: with a contact grill you can leave your pudding to bake while you eat the main course. Just take your choice from a selection of delicious desserts among the recipes here. Try a melt-in-the-mouth fruit pie or a crumble served sizzling hot from the grill to follow a cold meal, or prepare a cold dessert beforehand to succeed a hot main course. There's no limit to the variety you can offer and you'll have everyone calling for more.

And if your grill has a set of waffle plates, that's another dimension to add to the appetising dessert possibilities.

Mincemeat sponge pudding

Temperature: hottest setting · Serves: 4-6

50 g/2 oz self-raising flour
½ teaspoon baking powder
50 g/2 oz castor sugar
grated rind of 1 orange
50 g/2 oz soft margarine
1 egg
450 g/1 lb mincemeat

Place all the ingredients except the mincemeat in a bowl and beat together until soft, pale and light in texture. An electric food mixer will help save time. Spread the mincemeat over the bottom of the greased cooking tray and top with the sponge mixture, spreading evenly over the top. Cook on the hottest setting for 10 minutes until the sponge is risen and golden brown.

Variations

Lemon sponge pudding Use lemon rind instead of the orange rind and lemon curd instead of the mincemeat. Cook as above.

Jam pudding Omit the orange rind and use a layer of your favourite jam instead of the mincemeat. Cook as above.

Gingered rhubarb crumble

(Illustrated on page 86)
Temperature: hottest setting · Serves: 4

350 g/12 oz rhubarb, thinly sliced
2 pieces preserved stem ginger, chopped
100 g/4 oz castor sugar
100 g/4 oz plain flour
50 g/2 oz butter

Place the rhubarb, ginger and 75 g/3 oz of the sugar in the cooking tray. Sift the flour into a bowl and rub in the butter until the mixture resembles fine breadcrumbs. Stir in the rest of the sugar, then sprinkle this crumble mixture over the fruit and press down lightly. Cook on the hottest setting for 12-15 minutes. Serve hot with cream or vanilla ice cream, if liked.

Variations

Apple and date crumble Peel, core and slice 350 g/12 oz cooking apples and place in the cooking tray with 100 g/4 oz chopped cooking dates. Sprinkle over 75 g/3 oz castor sugar, or to taste. Make the crumble topping and cook as above.

Plum crumble Halve and stone 350 g/12 oz plums and place in the cooking tray with 75 g/3 oz castor sugar, or to taste. Make the crumble topping and cook as above.

Baked apples with raisin and orange sauce

(Illustrated on page 86)
Temperature: hottest setting · Serves: 4

2 cooking apples, peeled, halved and cored
50 g/2 oz soft light brown sugar
50 g/2 oz raisins
pared and chopped rind of 1 orange and juice of 2 oranges
2 tablespoons rum

Place the apple halves in the cooking tray, cut side down and sprinkle over the sugar, raisins and the orange rind and juice. Cook on the hottest setting for 8 minutes, until the apples are soft. Add the rum and serve immediately.

Baked apples with almond lemon sauce

Temperature: hottest setting · Serves: 4

Here is a variation on the above recipe that combines nutty almond flavours with tangy lemon.

2 cooking apples, peeled, halved and cored
50 g/2 oz soft light brown sugar
50 g/2 oz flaked almonds
pared and chopped rind and juice of 1 lemon
few drops almond essence
4 tablespoons port

Place the apple halves in the cooking tray, cut side down and sprinkle over the sugar, almonds, the lemon rind and juice and almond essence to taste. Cook on the hottest setting for 8 minutes, until the apples are soft. Add the port to the sauce and serve immediately with cream or natural yogurt, if liked.

Apple and cinnamon toasts

Temperature: hottest setting · Serves: 2

50 g/2 oz castor sugar
½ teaspoon ground cinnamon
50 g/2 oz butter
2 slices white bread, crusts removed
1 cooking apple, peeled and cored

Combine the sugar with the cinnamon. Spread half the butter
on one side of each bread slice and place in the cooking tray,
butter-side down. Slice the apple thickly and arrange the
slices on the bread. Sprinkle the cinnamon sugar thickly over
the apples and dot with the remaining butter. Cook on the
hottest setting for 15 minutes, until the sugar has caramelised
and the apples are soft. Serve with whipped cream or yogurt.

Summer lemon slices

(Illustrated on page 86)
Temperature: hottest setting · Serves: 4

*This recipe is ideal for serving on hot summer days. Serve
small, thoroughly chilled portions with clotted cream for a
light, tangy dessert.*

2 large lemons, thickly sliced
100 g/4 oz castor sugar
4 tablespoons lemon juice
1 tablespoon crème de menthe
sprigs of mint to decorate

Lay the lemon slices in the cooking tray and sprinkle with the
sugar and lemon juice. Cook on the hottest setting for 15
minutes until the lemons are tender. Cool, then stir in the
crème de menthe. Place the slices with the juice in four
shallow individual dishes and chill thoroughly. Decorate
each dish with a sprig of mint and serve with clotted cream.

Cherry cream pancakes

Temperature: hottest setting · Makes: approximately 10

Reversible cooking plates are a feature of many contact grills and the smooth griddle side is ideal for cooking pancakes. This method differs slightly from cooking pancakes in a frying pan as the batter is spread into a circle on the lightly-oiled griddle plate.

Pancakes
100 g/4 oz plain flour
pinch of salt
1 egg, lightly beaten
300 ml/½ pint milk
a little oil
Filling
1 (425-g/15-oz) can stoned black cherries
300 ml/½ pint double cream
1 tablespoon icing sugar

To make the pancakes, sift the flour into a bowl with the salt. Add the egg and gradually beat in the milk to give a smooth batter. Lightly brush the smooth griddle cooking plates with oil. Place a little of the batter on the plates and spread out using a palette knife to form a thin round pancake. Cook on the hottest setting until brown on the underside, about 2 minutes, then turn over and cook until lightly brown on the second side. Continue until all the batter is used up. Stack the finished pancakes with a little castor sugar sprinkled between each one to prevent sticking.

For the filling, drain the cherries, reserving the juice. Whip the cream with the icing sugar and 2 tablespoons of the cherry juice until stiff. Fold the cherries into the cream, divide the mixture between the pancakes and roll up. Serve immediately.

Waffles

Makes: approximately 10

*Waffles can be served simply with your favourite jam,
preserves or syrup. Alternatively, top them with fresh fruit
and sugar to taste. But, if you are feeling more adventurous,
try some of the topping suggestions given below.
Interchangeable waffle plates may be purchased for certain
contact grills, but if you really love waffles, invest in an
electric waffle iron.*

75 g/3 oz self-raising flour
50 g/2 oz butter
1 egg
300 ml/½ pint milk
pinch of salt

Sift the flour into a bowl and rub in the butter to resemble
fine breadcrumbs. Whisk the egg and milk together and
gradually beat in the flour and salt to give a smooth batter.

Using the waffle plates, pour enough batter in to cover the
plates and cook for 3 minutes until golden. Serve with any of
the following toppings:

Orange cinnamon syrup Mix together 6 tablespoons golden
syrup with the grated rind of 1 orange and ½ teaspoon of
ground cinnamon. Pour over the warm or cooled waffles.

Strawberry cream Whip 150 ml/¼ pint double cream with 2
tablespoons icing sugar until stiff. Fold in 225 g/8 oz hulled
and halved strawberries. Serve with cooled waffles for a
refreshing summer treat.

Bananas and brown sugar Slice 4 bananas and sprinkle with 4
tablespoons lemon juice to prevent discoloration. Add 2
tablespoons soft brown sugar and 150 ml/¼ pint double
cream. Pour over the waffles to serve.

Apple and honey Mix 2 peeled, cored and sliced dessert
apples with 1 tablespoon of lemon juice and 4 tablespoons of
honey. Serve with warm or cold waffles.

Baked cheesecake

Temperature: hottest setting · Serves: 6-8

This rich and filling cheesecake is ideal for freezing. Cut into individual portions and freeze in a rigid container. It will defrost quickly and makes a wonderful teatime treat.

Hazelnut base
100 g/4 oz plain flour
100 g/4 oz butter, softened
25 g/1 oz sugar
50 g/2 oz hazelnuts, finely chopped
Topping
grated rind of 2 lemons and juice of 1 lemon
100 g/4 oz castor sugar
450 g/1 lb cream cheese
50 g/2 oz raisins
2 tablespoons self-raising flour
2 eggs, lightly beaten

To make the hazelnut base, mix together the flour, butter, sugar and hazelnuts with a wooden spoon to make a soft dough. Press this dough into the base of the cooking tray and chill until firm.

For the topping, put the lemon rind and juice in a bowl with the sugar, cream cheese, raisins, flour and eggs. Beat until smooth. Spread this mixture over the chilled hazelnut base and cook on the hottest setting for 12-15 minutes, or until the mixture is set and well browned. If the top turns very brown before the cheesecake is cooked through, cover loosely with a piece of cooking foil. Allow the cheesecake to cool before removing it from the tray and chill well before serving.

Nut and banana date flan

Temperature: hottest setting · Serves: 6

Sweet shortcrust pastry
225 g/8 oz plain flour
175 g/6 oz butter
50 g/2 oz castor sugar
1 egg yolk
Filling
4 bananas
juice of 1 lemon
50 g/2 oz cooking dates, chopped
50 g/2 oz walnuts, chopped
2 tablespoons castor sugar
150 ml/¼ pint double cream, whipped

To make the pastry, sift the flour into a bowl and rub in the butter until the mixture resembles fine breadcrumbs. Sprinkle in the sugar, add the egg yolk and mix to form a soft dough. Knead lightly until smooth, wrap in cling film and chill until firm enough to roll. Roll out on a lightly-floured board or work surface and use to line the cooking tray.

For the filling, peel and slice the bananas thinly and toss in the lemon juice to prevent discoloration. Lay the slices in the pastry case and sprinkle over the dates, walnuts and sugar. Cook on the hottest setting for 15 minutes. Leave until just warm, then cut into individual portions and decorate with piped whipped cream, or serve the cream separately.

Mocha roulade

Temperature: hottest setting · Serves: 4-6

2 eggs
50 g/2 oz castor sugar
40 g/1½ oz plain flour
15 g/½ oz cocoa powder
2 teaspoons instant coffee powder
1 tablespoon boiling water
1 tablespoon icing sugar
300 ml/½ pint double cream
4 tablespoons chocolate vermicelli
chocolate buttons to decorate

Whisk the eggs with the sugar until pale and thick. Sift together the flour and cocoa powder and fold into the egg mixture. Line the cooking tray with greaseproof paper and grease well. Turn the whisked mixture into it and cook on the hottest setting for 5 minutes. Turn out on to a sheet of greaseproof paper on top of a clean tea towel. Trim the edges of the cake and place a second sheet of greaseproof paper on top. While still warm, carefully roll up using the tea towel, to enclose the top sheet of greaseproof paper and leave until cool.

Dissolve the coffee in the boiling water, add the icing sugar and double cream and whip until stiff. Unroll the chocolate roulade and remove the greaseproof paper. Spread thickly with some of the coffee cream and re-roll. Cover the outside of the roll with more cream and press the vermicelli over it. Pipe any remaining cream along the top of the cake and decorate with chocolate buttons.

BISCUITS & CAKES

It may surprise you to find how easy it is to make cakes, scones and biscuits in a contact grill but this is one of its greatest assets for the bedsit cook or the family with limited facilities. Cakes rise well and can be cut in half for filling; packet mixes are quick to prepare and easy to bake, and an empty biscuit tin is no disaster when you can replenish it in a matter of minutes.

If you want to make scones or drop scones, just open out the grill and reverse the plates to form a griddle. The recipes given here include a wide choice of teatime favourites and with the aid of your grill you can bake enough goodies to satisfy a hungry family.

Raspberry gâteau

2 eggs
50 g/2 oz castor sugar
50 g/2 oz plain flour
15 g/½ oz butter, melted
300 ml/½ pint double cream
225 g/8 oz raspberries
1 tablespoon icing sugar
1 tablespoon sweet sherry
50 g/2 oz roasted hazelnuts, chopped

Whisk the eggs with the sugar until pale and thick. Carefully fold in the flour and melted butter. Line the cooking tray with greaseproof paper and grease well. Turn the whisked egg mixture into it and cook on the hottest setting for 5 minutes. Turn out, remove the greaseproof paper and cool on a wire rack.

Whip the cream until stiff. Reserve a few raspberries for decoration and toss the remainder with the icing sugar. Sprinkle the sherry over the cooked cake and cut vertically down the middle. Spread some of the cream over half the cake, top with the sugared raspberries and place the second piece of cake on top. Spread some cream around the sides and over the top of the cake. Press the hazelnuts around the sides and pipe the remaining cream around the edge of the cake. Decorate with the reserved raspberries.

Variation

(Illustrated on page 104)

Cherry gâteau Substitute 375 g/12 oz stoned cherries for the raspberries and omit the icing sugar. Reserve two or three whole fruits for decoration.

Lemon cake

Temperature: hottest setting

75 g/3 oz self-raising flour
½ teaspoon baking powder
pinch of salt
75 g/3 oz castor sugar
grated rind of 1 lemon
75 g/3 oz soft margarine
1 large egg
100 g/4 oz lemon curd
Lemon glacé icing
100 g/4 oz icing sugar
1-2 tablespoons lemon juice
pared rind of 2 lemons to decorate

Sift the flour, baking powder and salt into a bowl. Add the sugar, lemon rind, margarine and egg and beat thoroughly, preferably with an electric food mixer, until soft and pale. Turn into the greased cooking tray and smooth over the top. Cook on the hottest setting for 7 minutes until risen and golden brown. Turn out to cool on a wire rack.

Cut the cold cake vertically down the middle and sandwich the two pieces together with the lemon curd. To make the lemon glacé icing, sift the icing sugar into a bowl and stir in enough lemon juice to give a thick pouring consistency. Pour the icing over the top of the cake, allowing it to flow down the sides. Decorate with thin strips of lemon rind.

Variation

Victoria sandwich Omit the lemon rind from the mixture and cook as above. Sandwich the cake together with raspberry jam instead of lemon curd and sift a little icing sugar over the top before serving.

Chocolate orange cake

Temperature: hottest setting

65 g/2½ oz self-raising flour
15 g/½ oz cocoa powder
1 teaspoon baking powder
pinch of salt
75 g/3 oz castor sugar
1 large egg
75 g/3 oz soft margarine
grated rind of 1 orange and juice of ½ orange
Buttercream
100 g/4 oz butter, softened
175 g/6 oz icing sugar, sifted
juice of ½ orange
100 g/4 oz hazelnuts, roasted and chopped
chocolate caraque or grated chocolate to decorate

Sift the flour into a bowl with the cocoa, baking powder and salt. Add the sugar, egg, margarine, orange rind and juice and beat until soft and creamy. Turn into the greased cooking tray and spread out evenly. Cook on the hottest setting for 7 minutes until risen and browned. Turn out to cool on a wire rack.

To make the buttercream, beat the butter in a bowl with the icing sugar until soft and pale. Gradually beat in the orange juice. Cut the cake vertically down the middle and sandwich the two halves together with some of the buttercream. Spread a little of the buttercream around the sides of the cake and press on the chopped nuts. Place the cake on a serving dish and spread some of the remaining cream over the top. Fit a piping bag with a star-shaped nozzle, fill with the remaining buttercream and pipe around the edge of the cake. Decorate the top with the chocolate caraque or grated chocolate.

Variation

For an even more elaborate dessert, use 300 ml/$\frac{1}{2}$ pint whipped double cream instead of the buttercream and decorate the top of the cake with slices of fresh fruit dipped in lemon juice to prevent discoloration.

Coconut crunchies

Temperature: hottest setting · Makes: 16

2 egg whites
50 g/2 oz castor sugar
100 g/4 oz coconut flour
grated rind of 1 lemon and 1 orange

In a bowl, whisk the egg whites until stiff. Gradually whisk in the sugar and continue to whisk until the mixture is thick and glossy. Stir in the coconut flour and lemon and orange rind. Place small spoonfuls of the mixture on the greased cooking tray and cook on the hottest setting for 7 minutes. Cool on a wire rack.

Variation

Ginger crunchies Add 50 g/2 oz finely-chopped crystallised ginger and the grated rind of 1 lemon to the coconut flour and orange rind. Continue as above.

Swiss roll

Temperature: hottest setting

2 eggs
50 g/2 oz castor sugar
50 g/2 oz plain flour
75 g/3 oz raspberry jam
castor sugar to sprinkle

Line the cooking tray with greaseproof paper and grease well. Whisk the eggs with the sugar until pale and creamy. Sift the flour and fold into the whisked mixture using a metal spoon. Turn into the lined cooking tray and cook on the hottest setting for 5 minutes.

Turn the cake out on to a sheet of greaseproof paper on a tea towel. Working quickly before the cake cools, trim off the edges and spread with the jam. Use the tea towel to help roll up the cake quickly and tightly. Allow to cool and sprinkle with castor sugar before serving.

Variation

Orange roll Add the grated rind of 1 large orange to the mixture with the dry ingredients and use orange marmalade instead of the jam. Dust with icing sugar before serving.

Clockwise: *Ham and tomato baps and Mozzarella sardines (page 122); Cheese pâté fingers (page 121); Prawn and ham, Turkey and cranberry toasted sandwiches (page 114); Apple and celery salad (page 124).*

Cherry flapjacks

(Illustrated on page 104)
Temperature: hottest setting · Makes: 12

175 g/6 oz rolled oats
2 tablespoons plain flour
75 g/3 oz golden syrup
75 g/3 oz butter, softened
50 g/2 oz glacé cherries, halved

In a bowl mix the rolled oats with the flour. Add the syrup, softened butter and cherries and mix thoroughly. Using the back of a spoon, press into the greased cooking tray and cook on the hottest setting for 10 minutes. Cut into squares while still warm and cool on a wire rack.

Date cookies

Temperature: hottest setting · Makes: 12

100 g/4 oz plain flour
75 g/3 oz butter
75 g/3 oz castor sugar
grated rind of 1 orange
50 g/2 oz dates, chopped
1 egg yolk

Sift the flour into a bowl and rub in the butter until the mixture resembles fine breadcrumbs. Add the remaining ingredients and mix to form a soft dough. Form into a roll measuring 3·5 cm/1½ inches in diameter and chill thoroughly. Slice into 12 pieces and place each slice well apart on the greased cooking tray. Cook on the hottest setting for 8-10 minutes. Cool slightly in the cooking tray then remove to cool on a wire rack.

Top: Cherry gâteau (page 98); Shortbread (page 107);
Scones (page 109); Cherry flapjacks (page 105).

Sultana and walnut squares

Temperature: hottest setting · Makes: 12

100 g/4 oz self-raising flour
½ teaspoon baking powder
pinch of salt
75 g/3 oz castor sugar
grated rind of 1 orange
75 g/3 oz soft margarine
1 large egg
50 g/2 oz sultanas
50 g/2 oz walnuts, chopped
Topping
100 g/4 oz plain chocolate
100 g/4 oz walnuts, chopped

Sift the flour, baking powder and salt into a bowl. Add all the remaining cake ingredients and beat thoroughly, until soft and pale, preferably using an electric food mixer. Turn into the greased cooking tray and spread out evenly. Cook on the hottest setting for 7 minutes until risen and golden. Turn out to cool on a wire rack.

To make the topping, melt the chocolate in a bowl over a saucepan of simmering water. Mix in the walnuts. Cut the cake into 12 squares and spread each square with some of the chocolate and nut mixture. Allow the topping to cool before serving.

Variation

Cherry squares Substitute 100 g/4 oz chopped glacé cherries for the sultanas and walnuts. Omit the orange rind and cook as above.

Shortbread

(Illustrated on page 104)
Temperature: medium setting · Makes: 20

175 g/6 oz butter, softened
75 g/3 oz icing sugar, sifted
250 g/9 oz plain flour
icing sugar to dust

In a bowl, cream the butter with the sugar until pale and creamy. Sift the flour and stir into the creamed mixture. Using the back of a spoon, press the mixture into the greased cooking tray and prick all over with a fork. Chill thoroughly for approximately 2 hours. Cook on a medium setting for 20 minutes. Cut the shortbread in half, lengthways and then cut into fingers while still hot. Leave to cool for a few minutes in the tray then remove to cool on a wire rack. Dust with icing sugar before serving.

Variation

Chocolate coated shortbread Finely chop 100 g/4 oz walnuts and sprinkle over the top of the shortbread before cooking. When cooked and cooled, coat the top with 175 g/6 oz melted plain chocolate.

Easy crumpets

Temperature: hottest setting · Makes: approximately 12

Unfortunately, crumpets are rarely made at home these days because of the time and effort involved in making and proving the batter. This recipe takes a short cut and uses bought bread mix which greatly reduces the preparation and proving time. The cooked results are mouthwatering!

275 g/10 oz white bread mix
300 ml/$\frac{1}{2}$ pint hand-hot milk
150 ml/$\frac{1}{4}$ pint hand-hot water
$\frac{3}{4}$ teaspoon bicarbonate of soda
a little oil

Place the bread mix in a bowl, make a well in the middle and pour in the milk. Gradually stir the bread mix into the milk using a wooden spoon. Add the water slowly, beating thoroughly to prevent lumps and to give a smooth thick batter. Cover with cling film and leave in a warm place for 20 minutes until frothy.

Sprinkle the bicarbonate of soda over the batter and beat well. Thoroughly grease the inside of 2 or more 7·5-cm/3-inch round metal pastry cutters and place on the lightly-oiled griddle plates. Spoon the batter into the rings to a depth of 1 cm/$\frac{1}{2}$ inch and cook on the hottest setting for 2-3 minutes until set around the edge and very bubbly on top. Use a knife to ease off the rings carefully around the crumpets, holding them with a tea towel. Turn over and cook on the other side without the rings until brown. Continue until all the batter mix is used. Serve hot with plenty of butter or turn out to cool on a wire rack and reheat in the cooking tray on the hottest setting for 2-3 minutes, when required.

Scones

(Illustrated on page 104)
Temperature: hottest setting · Makes: 8

100 g/4 oz self-raising flour
1 teaspoon baking powder
pinch of salt
25 g/1 oz butter
1 tablespoon castor sugar
4-5 tablespoons milk
milk to brush

Sift the flour into a bowl with the baking powder and salt. Rub in the butter until the mixture resembles fine breadcrumbs, then add the sugar and milk and mix to a soft dough. Knead gently on a lightly-floured board or work surface and then roll out to 1 cm/½ inch thick. Using a biscuit cutter, cut 8 (3·5 – 5-cm/1½ – 2-inch) rounds and place them in the greased cooking tray. Brush with a little milk and cook on the hottest setting for 8 minutes. Cool slightly then serve warm with butter, strawberry jam, or jam and clotted cream.

Variations

Cheese scones Omit the sugar. Add 40 g/1½ oz finely-grated Cheddar cheese and 1 tablespoon dry mustard to the dry ingredients. Continue as above but glaze the scones with a little beaten egg instead of milk.

Herbed bacon scones Omit the sugar. Add 2 teaspoons chopped mixed fresh herbs and 2 lean bacon rashers, rinds removed and chopped, to the dry ingredients. Continue as for basic scones, but glaze with a little beaten egg instead of milk. Serve hot with butter, cream cheese and a variety of salads.

Sultana scones Add 50 g/2 oz sultanas to the dry ingredients. Continue as for basic scones.

Drop scones

Temperature: hottest setting · Makes: approximately 24

100 g/4 oz self-raising flour
¼ teaspoon cream of tartar
25 g/1 oz butter, melted
1 egg
300 ml/½ pint milk
butter and castor sugar to serve

Sift the flour and cream of tartar into a bowl. Add the melted butter and egg and beat to give a smooth batter, gradually adding the milk.

Drop spoonfuls of the batter on to the lightly-greased griddle plates and cook on the hottest setting until bubbles appear on the surface of the batter, about 3 minutes. Turn the scones over and cook until browned underneath. Serve immediately with butter and a sprinkling of castor sugar. Alternatively, these scones may be served with Savoury butters (see pages 117-118).

Variation

Cottage cheese and ham drop scones Though traditionally a tea-time treat, drop scones can easily be adapted to make a simple and satisfactory supper dish. Use the above ingredients to make 4 large scones and cook in the same way. Meanwhile, mix together 225 g/8 oz cottage cheese, 225 g/8 oz diced cooked ham, 2 tablespoons chopped mixed fresh herbs and a few chopped spring onions. Top the scones with this mixture and serve immediately.

SANDWICHES & SNACKS

Your contact grill really comes into its own when between-meals snacks are wanted. Rushing in from work, a quick bite before the cinema; hungry children back from school, straight out to play; peckish in the night, mustn't wake the family – these are some of the crisis occasions when your grill comes to the rescue. Toasted sandwiches and instant snacks fill the gap when there's not enough time to heat up the oven or prepare a proper meal.

Here are some suggestions for appetising savouries and satisfying snacks. Also included are ideas for open sandwiches, and you will find instructions on how to make toasted sandwiches over the page.

TOASTED SANDWICHES

(Illustrated on page 103)

The versatility of the toasted sandwich is limited only by the cook's imagination and the requirements of the occasion. Both grill and sandwich maker are ideally suited for the preparation of a sustaining snack which can be prepared at any time of day or night. Sandwiches with runny fillings are best made between the specially provided deep sandwich plates of a sandwich maker, whereas sandwiches with more solid fillings can be cooked between the grilling plates of a contact grill. They should be served immediately or they will lose their crispness, and those with savoury fillings may be accompanied by a side salad, pickles or chutneys.

All kinds of bread can be used for sandwiches: rye, wholemeal, granary or pitta bread. The slices should be of medium thickness to allow the heat to penetrate and thoroughly cook the filling. Some of our own favourite variations on filling themes are on the following pages, but almost any savoury sandwich filling – tomato, bacon, sausage, cheese, ham or tuna fish – may be used. Sweet fillings, too, such as jam or fruit, make delicious sandwiches, and you can spread the bread with softened butter or any of the Savoury or Sweet butters suggested here. Depending on the filling, a toasted sandwich will take about 3 minutes to cook.

Appetising toasted sandwiches can also be made from leftovers and from many convenience foods such as spreads, canned meats or fish and creamed vegetables. Many fillings are suitable for freezing, so enabling a large number of sandwiches to be made in advance and frozen uncooked. When cooked from the frozen state, these will take about 5 to 7 minutes to toast, depending on the filling.

In addition to the conventional sandwiches, some ideas are also offered here for open sandwiches and for one or two quickly prepared snacks, such as Mozzarella sardines and Mushroom and bacon toasts, which make good starters.

To make a toasted sandwich, spread two slices of bread

with butter and sandwich any of the suggested fillings between them. Press the slices of bread together firmly, place each sandwich directly between the cooking plates and cook for 3 minutes on the hottest setting until the outside of the bread is crisp and golden. Serve immediately.

Each of the following recipes for fillings is sufficient to make two sandwiches.

Savoury fillings

Ham and cheese

25 g/1 oz Savoury butter (see pages 117-118)
2 thick slices cooked ham
50 g/2 oz cheese, sliced
(suitable for freezing)

Bacon and mushroom

25 g/1 oz Herby garlic butter (see page 117)
2 lean bacon rashers, rind removed and halved
50 g/2 oz mushrooms, sliced

Salami and apple

25 g/1 oz Herby garlic butter (see page 117)
6 slices salami
1 small eating apple, peeled, cored and sliced

Tuna and tomato

25 g/1 oz Lemon parsley butter (see page 117)
1 (99-g/3½-oz) can tuna, drained
1 tomato, peeled and sliced
salt and freshly ground black pepper

Lemon sardine

25 g/1 oz Lemon parsley butter (see page 117)
1 (120-g/4½-oz) can sardines, drained and mashed

Herby chicken

25 g/1 oz Herby garlic butter (see page 117)
100 g/4 oz cooked chicken, diced
50 g/2 oz full fat soft cheese, diced
(suitable for freezing)

Prawn and ham

25 g/1 oz Garlic butter (see page 117)
2 thin slices cooked ham
100 g/4 oz peeled cooked prawns
(suitable for freezing)

Turkey and cranberry

25 g/1 oz softened butter
1 tablespoon cranberry sauce
100g/4 oz cooked turkey, diced

Apple and blue cheese

25 g/1 oz Garlic butter (see page 117)
1 eating apple, peeled, cored and sliced
100 g/4 oz Stilton cheese, sliced

Garlic sausage and mushroom cream

25 g/1 oz Mixed herb butter (see page 117)
4 slices garlic sausage
50 g/2 oz button mushrooms, chopped
50 g/2 oz full fat soft cheese, diced

Chicken and corn

25 g/1 oz St Clement's butter (see page 117)
100 g/4 oz cooked chicken, diced
4 tablespoons canned sweet corn kernels
50 g/2 oz full fat soft cheese

Curried chicken

25 g/1 oz Peanut butter (see page 118)
100 g/4 oz cooked chicken, chopped
1 teaspoon concentrated curry paste
50 g/2 oz full fat soft cheese
(suitable for freezing)

Cottage cheese and bacon

25 g/1 oz Anchovy butter (see page 118)
2 lean bacon rashers, rind removed and halved
50 g/2 oz cottage cheese

Sage Derby and pear

25 g/1 oz butter
50 g/2 oz sage Derby cheese, grated
1 small pear, peeled, cored and sliced

Quick chicken and cucumber

1 (53-g/1⅞-oz) pot chicken spread
1 small onion, finely chopped
¼ small cucumber, peeled and finely diced
salt and freshly ground black pepper

Salmon relish

1 (53-g/1⅞-oz) pot salmon pâté
1 tablespoon sweet corn relish
4 spring onions, finely chopped
generous pinch of nutmeg

Devilled crab

1 (53-g/1⅞-oz) pot crab spread
1 teaspoon concentrated tomato purée
½ teaspoon French mustard
50 g/2 oz cheese, grated
dash of Worcestershire sauce

Bierwurst club sandwich

6 thin slices bread
50 g/2 oz Blue cheese butter (see opposite page)
8 thin slices Bierwurst sausage

Spread the bread thinly with some of the Blue cheese butter and sandwich together with the Bierwurst. Spread the remaining butter on the outside of the club sandwich and cook directly between the cooking plates on the hottest setting for 3 minutes.

Sweet fillings

Banana and brown sugar

25 g/1 oz St Clement's butter (see opposite page)
1 banana, peeled and sliced
1 tablespoon soft brown sugar

Cream cheese and jam

50 g/2 oz full fat soft cheese
1 tablespoon jam

Apple and cinnamon

25 g/1 oz Cinnamon butter (see page 118)
1 eating apple, peeled, cored and sliced

Apple and raisin

25 g/1 oz Honey butter (see page 118)
25 g/1 oz raisins, chopped
1 eating apple, peeled, cored and sliced

Savoury butters

Beat any of the following ingredients into 100 g/4 oz of softened butter. The flavoured butters may be stored in the refrigerator wrapped in cooking foil for up to 2 weeks or frozen for 2-3 months.

Mixed herb butter

4 tablespoons chopped mixed fresh herbs
salt and freshly ground black pepper

Lemon parsley butter

2 tablespoon chopped parsley
grated rind of 2 lemons
salt and freshly ground black pepper

Garlic butter

2 cloves garlic, crushed
salt and freshly ground black pepper

Herby garlic butter

4 tablespoons chopped mixed fresh herbs
1 clove garlic, crushed
grated rind of 1 lemon
salt and freshly ground black pepper

St Clement's butter

grated rind of 1 orange
grated rind of 2 lemons
salt and freshly ground black pepper
or 2 teaspoons icing sugar

Blue cheese butter

100 g/4 oz Danish blue cheese, or similar blue cheese

Peanut butter

100 g/4 oz ground peanuts

Emmenthal butter

100 g/4 oz Emmenthal cheese, finely grated

Mustard butter

2 tablespoons wholegrain mustard

Anchovy butter

1 (56-g/2-oz) can anchovies, drained and mashed
grated rind of 1 lemon

Spiced butter

2 teaspoons ground mixed spice
1 clove garlic, crushed
salt and freshly ground black pepper

Sweet butters

Cinnamon butter

1 tablespoon ground cinnamon
1 tablespoon castor sugar

Marmalade butter

3 tablespoons marmalade

Honey butter

2 tablespoons thick honey

SNACKS

Parmesan eggs

Temperature: hottest setting · Serves: 4

2 Vienna rolls, halved
4 small eggs
2 tablespoons grated Parmesan cheese
salt and freshly ground black pepper
chopped parsley to garnish

Scoop out and discard all the soft bread from the rolls. Carefully crack an egg into each bread shell and top with Parmesan cheese. Season lightly and place in the cooking tray. Cook on the hottest setting for 10 minutes. Sprinkle with chopped parsley before serving.

Variations

Eggs with anchovies Substitute 1 (56-g/2-oz) can anchovy fillets, drained for the cheese. Top each egg with chopped anchovy fillets and cook as above. Sprinkle with chopped parsley before serving.
Eggs with garlic sausage Substitute 100 g/4 oz finely-chopped garlic sausage for the Parmesan cheese. Cook as above.

Welsh rarebit

Temperature: hottest setting · Serves: 2-4

Traditionally, Welsh rarebit is made with ale and the cheese mixture is melted in a saucepan before being spread on hot toast and browned under the grill. This variation is easier, yet equally delicious, particularly when served with grilled bacon. Whisky is an interesting alternative to ale as it gives an unusually tangy flavour.

175 g/6 oz Caerphilly cheese, finely grated
1 teaspoon wholegrain mustard
salt and freshly ground black pepper
2 tablespoons brown ale, whisky or milk
4 thick slices bread
1 sliced tomato and sprigs of parsley to garnish

In a bowl, mix the cheese with the mustard and season generously. Gradually beat in the ale, whisky or milk to give a smooth, creamy mixture. Remove the crusts from the bread, if liked, then spread the cheese mixture over one side of each slice. Place the slices in the cooking tray, cheese side up, and cook on the hottest setting for 5 minutes, until the cheese has melted. Top with slices of tomato and sprigs of parsley and serve immediately.

Variations

Herb rarebit Add 2 tablespoons chopped fresh herbs to the cheese mixture. Cook as above.
Onion and tomato rarebit Add 1 finely-chopped small onion and 1 tablespoon concentrated tomato purée to the cheese mixture. Cook as above.
Tuna rarebit Drain and flake 1 (198-g/7-oz) can tuna and mix with 4 finely-chopped spring onions and the grated rind of 1 lemon. Top each slice of cooked Welsh rarebit with this mixture and serve immediately.

Sweet corn and pepper rarebit Deseed and chop 1 small green pepper and 1 small red pepper. Drain 1 (198-g/7-oz) can sweet corn kernels and mix with the peppers. Top the uncooked slices of Welsh rarebit with this mixture and cook as above.

Prawn and olive rarebit Mix 100 g/4 oz peeled cooked prawns with 100 g/4 oz sliced stuffed green olives and use to top each cooked slice of Welsh rarebit. Garnish with lemon wedges and serve immediately.

Cheese pâté fingers

(Illustrated on page 103)
Temperature: hottest setting · Makes: 8

100 g/4 oz Danish blue cheese
100 g/4 oz coarse pâté
4 finger rolls
lemon wedges to garnish

In a bowl, cream the cheese and combine with the pâté until thoroughly mixed. Split the rolls in half and spread each half with some of the cheese mixture. Place in the cooking tray and cook on the hottest setting for 5 minutes until the rolls and topping are hot but not browned. Garnish with small wedges of lemon and serve with a mixed salad.

Variations

Creamed pâté fingers Substitute 100 g/4 oz full fat soft cheese for the blue cheese. Cook as above.

Cheese and ham fingers Substitute 100 g/4 oz chopped cooked ham for the pâté. Cream the blue cheese with 50 g/ 2 oz full fat soft cheese, then add the ham and cook as above.

Mozzarella sardines

(Illustrated on page 103)
Temperature: hottest setting · Serves: 4

2 baps
100 g/4 oz Mozzarella cheese, sliced
2 (120-g/4¼-oz) cans sardines in oil, drained
salt and freshly ground black pepper
grated rind of 1 lemon
lemon slices and sprigs of parsley to garnish

Halve each bap and top each half with the cheese. Arrange
the whole sardines on top, season generously and sprinkle
with lemon rind. Place in the cooking tray and cook on the
hottest setting for 3-5 minutes until the cheese has melted.
Garnish with lemon slices and sprigs of parsley.

Variations

Frankfurter and pineapple baps Top each halved bap with
the cheese, as above. Substitute 225 g/8 oz sliced Frankfurter
sausages and 4 canned and drained pineapple rings for the
sardines and lemon rind. Cook as above and garnish with
watercress.

Ham and tomato baps Substitute 4 slices of cooked ham and 2
tomatoes for the sardines and lemon rind. Halve the slices of
ham, roll up each piece and secure with a wooden cocktail
stick. Quarter the tomatoes and arrange on the baps with the
ham. Cook as above. Remove the cocktail sticks before
serving.

Mushroom and bacon toasts

Temperature: hottest setting · Serves: 2

These savouries are ideal as a quick snack or make a tasty first course for a dinner party or a breakfast-time treat with a difference.

25 g/1 oz butter
½ teaspoon French mustard
2 thick slices bread
100 g/4 oz button mushrooms
salt and freshly ground black pepper
4 lean bacon rashers, rind removed

In a bowl, cream the butter with the mustard and spread on one side of each slice of bread. Place in the cooking tray, mustard side up, and top with the mushrooms. Season lightly. Halve the bacon rashers and place on top. Cook on the hottest setting for 10 minutes. Serve immediately.

Variations

Tomato and bacon toasts Substitute 2 sliced tomatoes for the mushrooms. Cook as above.
Avocado bacon toasts Omit the mustard. Peel and slice 1 ripe avocado and sprinkle with lemon juice to prevent discoloration. Arrange the avocado on the buttered bread, top with the bacon and cook as above. Garnish with lemon wedges and sprigs of parsley.

SIDE SALADS AND DRESSINGS

Tomato salad

450 g/1 lb tomatoes, peeled and roughly chopped
1 bunch spring onions, chopped
Honey dressing (see opposite page)

Place the tomatoes in a serving bowl with the onion and pour over the dressing. Toss lightly before serving.

Apple and celery salad

(Illustrated on page 103)

4 eating apples, cored and sliced
1 head celery, chopped
Mayonnaise dressing (see opposite page)
100 g/4 oz flaked almonds, toasted

In the serving bowl, mix the apple with the celery. Add the dressing and toss lightly. Top with the almonds and serve immediately.

Beetroot and bacon salad

225 g/8 oz lean bacon, chopped and cooked
4 large beetroot, cooked and diced
Mayonnaise dressing (see opposite page)
1 tablespoon chopped parsley

Drain the cooked bacon on absorbent kitchen paper. In a serving bowl, mix the bacon with the beetroot. Spoon over the dressing and sprinkle over the parsley to serve.

Honey dressing

2 tablespoons honey
4 tablespoons lemon juice
150 ml/¼ pint olive oil
salt and freshly ground black pepper
2 teaspoons whole grain mustard
1 clove garlic, crushed

Place all the ingredients in a screw-top jar and shake vigorously until smooth and well combined. This dressing may be stored in the refrigerator for up to 4 weeks. Shake well before use.

Mayonnaise dressing

150 ml/¼ pint mayonnaise
salt and freshly ground black pepper
2 teaspoons wholegrain mustard
grated rind of 1 lemon
1 teaspoon golden syrup
1 tablespoon lemon juice

Place all the ingredients in a small bowl and stir until thoroughly combined. Store in the refrigerator and use within 2 days.

Index